# ORGANIZATIONAL CHANGE
## The Effect of Successful Leadership

# THE IRWIN-DORSEY SERIES IN BEHAVIORAL SCIENCE IN BUSINESS

## EDITORIAL COMMITTEE

# ORGANIZATIONAL CHANGE
## The Effect of Successful Leadership

*by*

ROBERT H. GUEST, Ph.D.

PROFESSOR OF BUSINESS ADMINISTRATION
THE AMOS TUCK SCHOOL OF BUSINESS ADMINISTRATION
DARTMOUTH COLLEGE

A YALE TECHNOLOGY PROJECT PRODUCTION

1962
THE DORSEY PRESS, INC., AND
RICHARD D. IRWIN, INC., HOMEWOOD, ILLINOIS

# Foreword

The first two sentences of Robert Guest's introduction are a remarkable condensation—and characterization—of the book. "This is a study," Professor Guest writes, "of a patient who was acutely ill and who became extremely healthy. The 'patient' was not a Man but a Management, the management of a large complex industrial organization." From these few words can be deduced many of the useful and unique features of this book. To begin with, the subject is of great practical interest to leaders of industry and labor in an industrial civilization populated by thousands of "large complex industrial organizations"—not a few of which are acutely ill in one or another of their vital organs. But one can also deduce that the book is not merely a negative report of organizational fevers or failures, but that it contains diagnostic and therapeutic material. The patient "*became* extremely healthy."

Because I was fortunate in working closely with the author during the whole period of his research, I would like to tell something of the book's orgin, and of why—although the author's own view of his work is modest—it may mark the beginnings of a breakthrough in a relatively new but important area of social science research.

Research and most of the writing for the book was done while Professor Guest was with the Technology Project of Yale University. As early as 1947 he was associated with me in many research studies in large automobile plants, and out of these the opportunity presented itself in 1953 to begin the study on which this book is based. Like all other research of the Technology Project, it embodied three features: First, it was made in an on-going industrial organization; second, it gave full recognition to the importance of the technological component in the modern corporation; third, it was concerned with "problems of change."

But Robert Guest has succeeded both through his original research and in his final presentation of the material in adding certain unique characteristics. Some of these are suggested in the two opening sentences of the book. But more specifically and more completely they are these:

1. The book I believe is one of the few systematic studies of a large complex organization in *process of change*. The author has not only given "before and after" readings in the structure of the organization studied, but has focussed on the process of change itself, the discreet change phenomena which made the structure actually move from Form A to Form B. He has added, in other words, the dimension of duration to a study of organizational behavior undergoing change.

2. The book contains an unusually complete sheaf of performance indices which, from a certain point of view, may be said to be the administrative "resultant" of all the attitudinal and structural changes, which are also reported. The presence of this performance data, in complete reliable and meaningful form, is due to several factors. The first is sheer luck: the fact that a series of circumstances brought a competent research scientist at a strategic moment in touch with an *important* and *measurable* change. The second is the enlightened policy of management which generously provided both the research site and the statistical material. The third and perhaps the crucial factor was the dogged persistence, the tact and the skill of Robert Guest. He "asked"—persistently—and he "received," and what he received he translated into meaningful terms for both the lay and the professional reader.

3. The book exhibits full recognition of the technological environment within which an important change phenomenon occurred. Guest's own comment on this point is worth quoting: ". . . the social scientist often makes the error of concentrating on human motivation and group behavior without fully accounting for the technical environment which circumscribes, even determines the roles which the actors play. Moti-

vation, group structure, interaction processes, authority—none of these abstractions of behavior takes place in a technological vacuum."

4. Finally, the author has put what might have been merely a highly dramatic but purely empirical case history into a broad theoretical perspective.

Maps are still crude and rare for orienting the social scientist for travel through the research wilderness of complex organizations. Robert Guest's study gives accurately certain distances and contours for one patch in this wilderness. But the patch is important to administrator and scholar alike and it is surveyed in sufficient detail and with enough vision of the whole territory to be both a help and an encouragement to future explorers.

CHARLES R. WALKER
*Director,* Yale Technology Project

*More is learned from a single success than from multiple failures. A single success proves it can be done. Therefore, it is necessary to learn what made it work.*

R. K. MERTON

# Acknowledgments

Several scores of persons who gave so generously of their time to make this study possible cannot be named inasmuch as it was agreed that they should remain anonymous. These include the supervisors, union officers, personnel manager, and many others at Plant Y. I am especially indebted to the two plant managers and to officials of Corporation X.

To my Yale colleague of long standing, Charles R. Walker, go my deepest thanks. His impatience spurred me on and his patience helped immensely over the rough spots. My former colleagues, Professor Arthur N. Turner and Dr. Frank J. Jasinski, not only helped in the field work, but their own academic efforts set the standard for me. For both criticism and encouragement I am indebted to Professors Paul F. Lazarsfeld, Robert K. Merton, Conrad M. Arensberg at Columbia, and to the earlier inspiration of Professor Robert S. Lynd. Among the several scholars at Yale who frequently and willingly gave a helping hand, Professors E. Wight Bakke and Chris Argyris come to mind first. Professor John W. Hennessey, my present colleague at the Amos Tuck School of Business Administration at Dartmouth, made a number of useful suggestions.

The late Mary B. Clark cheerfully helped with the bibliographical references as did Emily C. Moore. O. Sandra Ray spent many hours on the index. Dorothy L. Badger responded above and beyond the call of duty in preparing the manuscript.

Funds for editing and final preparation time were made available from the Alfred P. Sloan Foundation to the Amos Tuck School.

R.H.G.

Hanover, New Hampshire
November, 1961

# Table of Contents

CHAPTER          PAGE

1. INTRODUCTION ....................................... 1

2. PLANT Y—ORGANIZATION AND TECHNOLOGY............... 9

A. BASIC ORGANIZATION STRUCTURE IN BOTH TIME PERIODS. B. BASIC TECH-
NICAL SYSTEM IN BOTH TIME PERIODS.

3. PLANT Y IN 1953—THE PERIOD OF DISINTEGRATION........... 17

A. VERTICAL RELATIONS IN THE PRODUCTION ORGANIZATION: 1. The Man-
ager's Relations to Superiors and Subordinates. 2. Subordinates' Relations to the
Plant Manager. 3. Superior/Subordinate Relations below the Plant Manager.
B. RELATION OF PRODUCTION TO NONPRODUCTION GROUPS: 1. Material and
Production Control. 2. Inspection. C. PLANT Y: PERFORMANCE—1953: 1. Effi-
ciency. 2. Quality Performance. 3. Indirect Labor Performance. 4. Safety
Record. 5. Labor Grievances. 6. Absenteeism. 7. Turnover.

4. PLANT Y FROM 1953 TO 1956............................ 40

A. THE SUCCESSION OF A NEW PLANT MANAGER. B. THE INTRODUCTION OF
MEETINGS. C. SHIFTS IN PERSONNEL. D. CHANGES IN THE TECHNICAL OR-
GANIZATION.

5. PLANT Y IN 1956.................................... 56

A. VERTICAL RELATIONS IN THE PRODUCTION ORGANIZATION: 1. General
Attitudinal Comments. 2. Subordinates' Relations with the Plant Manager.
3. Superior/Subordinate Relations below the Plant Manager. 4. Peer Relations
at the Foreman Level. B. RELATIONS OF PRODUCTION TO NONPRODUCTION
GROUPS: 1. Material Control. 2. Inspection. 3. Work Standards. 4. Maintenance
(Plant Engineering). 5. The Comptroller's Department.

6. BEFORE AND AFTER: PATTERNS OF INTERACTION, SENTIMENTS,

AND PERFORMANCE ................................ 82

A. INTERACTION: 1. The General Pattern. 2. Vertical Interactions. 3. Interaction
Patterns of Production to Nonproduction Groups. 4. Summary of Interaction
Patterns. B. SENTIMENTS. C. PERFORMANCE RESULTS: 1. General Efficiency.
2. Efficiency Loss and Recovery in Periods of Schedule Change. 3. Efficiency
Loss and Recovery in Periods of Model Change. 4. Indirect Labor Costs.
5. Quality Performance. 6. Safety Performance. 7. Labor Grievances. 8. Ab-
senteeism. 9. Turnover. 10. Summary of Performance. D. CONCLUDING RE-
MARKS ABOUT INTERACTION, SENTIMENTS, AND PERFORMANCE.

7. THE PROCESS OF CHANGE .............................. 106

A. CRITICAL CONDITIONS LEADING TO THE FIRST PHASE OF CHANGE. B. PHASES
IN THE CHANGE PROCESS: 1. The Succession of a New Manager. 2. The Man-
ager's Becoming Informed about the Needs of the Organization. 3. "Institu-
tionalizing" Interactions. 4. Enlarging the Span of Cognition. 5. Planning and
Action. 6. Reinforcement of Results. 7. Final Phase—Aftermath. C. OBSERVA-
TIONS.

8. THE NATURE OF AUTHORITY IN PERSPECTIVE ................ 118

A. THE PROBLEM OF DEFINING AUTHORITY AND DETERMINING ITS DERIVA-
TION. B. CONDITIONS OF EFFECTIVE AUTHORITY: 1. "Leeway to Act." 2. Time
Perspective. 3. Horizontal Work-Flow Interaction. 4. Enlarging the Span of
Cognition of the Leader and Subordinates. 5. Group Interaction.

9. PRODUCTION ORGANIZATIONS AS SOCIO-TECHNICAL SYSTEMS.... 134

APPENDIX. REVIEW OF RESEARCH........................... 138

A. SOURCES OF TENSION AND STRESS IN ORGANIZATIONS. B. THE PROCESS BY
WHICH STRAIN AND TENSION CAN BE MODIFIED. C. THE ROLE OF THE
LEADER IN THE PROCESS OF CHANGE.

BIBLIOGRAPHY ........................................ 161

AUTHOR INDEX ....................................... 173

SUBJECT INDEX ....................................... 175

# CHAPTER 1

# Introduction

This is a study of a patient who was acutely ill and who became extremely healthy. The "patient" was not a Man but a Management, the management of a large, complex industrial organization. It is a study of the process of change, not only in attitudes but also in the pattern of actions and relationships, which, in the span of three years, measurably altered the performance of the entire organization.

The author hopes that this empirical study of success will move us a bit farther down the road in the quest for a more sophisticated theory of organization and change. And if a few readers who are charged with the day-to-day responsibility of managing a complex organization should gain some new insights from this book, the writer will be satisfied.

The study of change in a complex human group is a relatively new field of theoretical inquiry. The initial breakthrough was made during the past decade when people from several different disciplines came to realize that no single discipline had a corner on the organization market. As Mason Haire observed: "It (the study of organization) is the natural focus of several disciplines"[1] including those involving game theory, small group phenomena, operations research, motivation theory, and many other approaches.

Sociologists have provided new stimulus in their interpretations and modifications of Max Weber's pioneering work on

---

[1] Mason Haire, "Introduction," in Mason Haire (ed.), *Modern Organization Theory*, p. 2.

bureaucracy. Anthropologists and social psychologists are to an increasing extent showing interest in the dynamics of large-scale organization. Even in business itself one occasionally finds a staff member working on organizational problems in the abstract with no immediate pragmatic purpose in mind.

What is lacking in this new area of scientific inquiry, in spite of the promising efforts of men like Bakke, Parsons, March, and Simon, to name a few, is a comprehensive framework within which to operate. Indeed, we may never reach this point. Unlike medical men after Harvey's great discovery on the circulatory system of the human body, we have no unifying concept around which to make further refinements and discoveries.

At this stage of development what is needed most—this is what the model builders and theorists usually say somewhere in a footnote—is more empirical material, more real life studies in on-going organizations. The important proviso is that the researcher work with at least a few theoretical hunches in mind. Interesting case studies are not enough. This writer would add a further proviso: understanding organizational dynamics by definition requires consideration of a time dimension. Useful hypotheses have been developed from recent research, yet it is becoming patently clear that not enough is known about the *process* by which a complex purposive group, such as a large industrial plant, shifts from a condition of failure to success over time. Arensberg, dissatisfied with descriptions of social systems and their static properties, urges the study of "specific events of specific persons in identifiable orders of stimulation in space and time."[2] Among several questions he poses are the following:

1. What degree of convergence must develop between the goals (values) of those persons being led and the goals of those planning and commanding?

---

[2] Conrad M. Arensberg, "Behavior and Organization: Industrial Studies," in John H. Rohrer and Muzafer Sherif (eds.), *Social Psychology at the Crossroads*, p. 349.

2. What activities of leadership initiate change, and once it has begun, what are the actions necessary to sustain it? [3]

Lack of data on the process of change over a time span leaves unanswered the question: "How is it possible to create an organization in which the individual may obtain optimum expression, and simultaneously in which the organization itself may obtain optimum satisfaction of its demands?" [4]

There is the need to understand the "conditions favorable to continuous adjustive development. We do not have sufficient empirical evidence to give a conclusive answer to this question." [5] Elsewhere, Blau observes with regret that "the empirical data for most studies were collected at one time, and the patterns of change had to be inferred subsequently." [6]

Gouldner's work in the gypsum plant was cleary concerned with problems of change and the relationship of leadership to bureaucratic functions. [7] Most of his major hypotheses at the end of the study implicitly call for further research on processes of change in on-going organizations over a span of time. Homans, with his emphasis on the mutual dependence of interaction, activity, and sentiment, urges continued research to substantiate his hypotheses concerning social structure in a "moving equilibrium." [8]

There are practical as well as conceptual problems of studying large, complicated socio-technical systems such as industrial plants. Managements are reluctant to open up their organizations to scrutiny by outsiders. Time and again this researcher has been told, "We don't like to have our dirty linen washed in public." When studies are made they are usually

---

[3] Conrad M. Arensberg and Geoffrey Tootell, "Plant Sociology: Real Dimensions and New Problems," in Mirra Komarovsky (ed.), *Common Frontiers of the Social Sciences*, p. 319. (Note: This is a paraphrase of original quote.)

[4] Chris Argyris, "The Individual and Organization: Some Problems of Mutual Adjustment," *Administrative Science Quarterly*, Vol. 2, No. 1 (June, 1957), p 3.

[5] Peter M. Blau, *Bureaucracy in Modern Society*, p. 60.

[6] Peter M. Blau, "Formal Organization: Dimensions of Analysis," *American Journal of Sociology*, Vol. 63, No. 1 (July, 1957), p. 69.

[7] Alvin W. Gouldner, *Patterns of Industrial Bureaucracy*.

[8] George C. Homans, *The Human Group*.

centered on the lower levels of the organization—on hourly and clerical workers. Probing the inner workings of management itself is still regarded as a kind of "classified" activity. It is not only that competitors might learn something: the results may be upsetting to the delicate power struggle which characterizes so many managerial groups.

On his part the social scientist often makes the error of concentrating on human motivation and group behavior without fully accounting for the technical environment which circumscribes, even determines, the roles which the actors play. Motivation, group structure, interaction processes, authority—none of these abstractions of behavior takes place in a technological vacuum.

This study is a modest attempt to meet some of the problems and shortcomings of research on change over time in complex organizations. During the early 1950's, this researcher and his colleagues at the Technology Project, Yale Institute of Human Relations, conducted a series of studies in two large automobile assembly plants. The general purpose of these studies was to determine how modern technological methods influenced intrinsic work satisfactions, and how the application of mass production principles influenced the pattern and quality of interpersonal relations among hourly workers and front line supervisors.[9]

In 1953 attention was focused on one of the plants (5,000 employees) because its performance compared with that of five other almost identical plants in the division was especially poor, at least by management's standards. Indeed, some members of this division and of the corporation at high levels were talking about the need to take drastic action; one even strongly recommended the closing of the plant.

During this period it was decided to study the whole managerial organization in order to find out the causes of the critical condition. Interviews were conducted with 28 foremen, 8 general foremen, and most members of high supervision, including

---

[9] For list of publications by the author and his colleagues, see Bibliography. Charles R. Walker is the Director of the Technology Project.

the plant manager and members of his staff in the production and nonproduction departments. A 15 per cent sample of hourly workers (218) had been interviewed in their homes previously. Many hours of observation and informal discussions were spent in the plant's major production departments. Interviews were also conducted with the division manager (in charge of 6 assembly plants), his staff, the corporation vice-president over 8 divisions (22 plants), and the executive vice-president over the operations of 126 plants. Also interviewed were local and international union officers. Background data on personnel and performance records were examined.

In mid-1953, as we began to study the findings, a new manager was assigned to the plant (it shall be referred to as Plant Y). Some interviews with members of the managerial group, including the new manager, were conducted at this time. During the next two and a half years, while continuing the analysis of the original study of Plant Y, occasional comments were heard to the effect that Plant Y was undergoing some profound changes.

Beginning in February, 1956, a new full-scale research program within the managerial group was started. More than 40 members of supervision, including most of those who had been seen earlier, were interviewed at length. Considerable time was spent with the plant manager and his staff. Records of performance, personnel, and technical changes were examined and other types of information were obtained from the division, corporation, and the union.

The decision to proceed was based not only on the apparent fact that performance and attitudes had undergone substantial change. Of crucial importance, for purposes of scientific inquiry, were certain controlling "constants" in the situation which made it possible to concentrate on what seemed to trigger the change—the succession of a new leader.

Specifically, it was found that during the entire period under the administration of the new manager:

1. The incumbents of offices in direct line of authority *above* the plant level—division manager, group vice-president, operating

executive vice-president, and corporation president—remained the same.

2. The plant itself operated with substantially the same supervisory personnel.
3. The formal structure of organization (number of levels, chain of command, span of control, and departmental functions) remained unchanged.
4. The plant continued to produce the same line of products under the same basic conditions of layout and technology.
5. Plant Y was subject to the same annual car model changes and to external market conditions that other similar plants had to face.

That these factors remained constant was fortunate. A change in one or more would have made it difficult if not impossible to account for the causes of change.

The project was undertaken then with the knowledge that:

1. Plant Y, under the former manager, had been in serious trouble. Not only was its performance poor, but expressions of bitter hostility and discouragement were heard at all levels of the organization.
2. In time these expressions of hostility and discouragement virtually disappeared, and the plant as a production organization appeared to function more efficiently not only by its own standards but also when compared with six other similar plants.
3. The change in attitudes and performance followed the introduction of a new manager.

Given these general observations, the task at hand was to discover what led to the change. This observer wanted to go beyond explaining immediate causes and manifest results. It was hoped that the findings would be useful as a sounding board against which to throw some broader theoretical questions about leadership and change in complex organizations.

The three broad statements above can be turned into questions of "why," and these questions will serve to structure the major parts of this book. After a descriptive chapter on Plant Y's organization and technology (Chapter 2), the periods of disintegration, of change, and of ultimate success are discussed in turn.

The body of material in the earlier descriptive sections is set down with the least amount of interpretation consistent with orderly presentation. The participants, members of the managerial group, "speak for themselves." In the following analytical and interpretive chapters we look first at what appear to be the essential differences in Time Period One and Time Period Two with respect to the patterns of communications (interactions) and the qualitative judgments (sentiments) which men expressed about themselves, their associates, and their total work environment. Critical examination is made of performance (measurable results of activities). Then a chapter is devoted to the *process* by which an organization shifts from one condition to another, followed by a chapter on the manager's role in this change process. A short section on organizations as socio-technical systems comes at the end. In these later chapters, the analysis draws from and, it is hoped, builds upon the work of others who have been concerned with change in complex organizations. A review of past research, in the Appendix, covers what others have said about (1) the sources of tension and stress which tend to militate against goal achievement in groups and organizations, (2) the process of change, and (3) the role of the primary agent (the leader) in bringing about change.

Let it be clear at the outset that this study is a naturalistic field observation which relies primarily on the inductive approach. It is not what Haire calls "the more rarified deduction from a relatively abstract model." [10] It is the writer's conviction that before we move too far in the construction of abstract models of human organization we need to learn more about the not-so-abstract way in which human beings actually behave in our complex industrial society.

Having said this it is worth emphasizing that this is something more than a case study as such. At several points in the analytical sections the author introduces theoretical ideas of

[10] Haire, *op. cit.*, p. 2.

others and examines them critically in light of the evidence. The results are reinforcements, modifications, combinations, and, sometimes, rejections of earlier concepts. This would appear to be the most reasonable approach for understanding complex organizations and change—an area of human inquiry still very much in its infancy.

# CHAPTER 2

# Plant Y—Organization and Technology

## A. BASIC ORGANIZATION STRUCTURE IN BOTH TIME PERIODS

Plant Y is but one unit of the total corporate organization. In terms of size, the corporation is comprised of more than a half million employees. There are more than 40 manufacturing divisions and over 126 plants in the United States. At the top of the organizational pyramid is the board of directors, responsible primarily to the stockholders. The chief executive is the president. Not including the many staff groups (financial, legal, etc.) reporting to the president, the direct line organization down through the several levels to the lowest level of management at Plant Y is as follows:

Chairman of the Board
President
Executive Vice-President
Divisional Group Vice-President
General Manager of the Division

Focus of Study
{
Plant Manager
Production Manager
General Superintendent
Department Superintendent
General Foreman
Foreman
}

Hourly Wage Earners

The plant manager and his subordinate supervisory organization down through the foreman level are our primary concern. However, in the total organization, the division manager to whom the plant manager reports is also important. The division manager was responsible in 1953 for six final assembly plants located in different areas of the country; a seventh plant was added to his jurisdiction in 1954. The division manager, in addition to having the several plant managers report to him, has a central staff responsible for certain functions in the over-all division of labor. They include such persons as the divisional comptroller, personnel director, head of quality control, head of work standards, and several others.

The plant manager, as in all plants in the division, also has a number of department heads reporting to him. There are ten in all, each in charge of certain functions generally comparable to those in any industrial plant. The plant manager's key subordinate is the production manager, who heads all of the operations directly connected with the assembly of the product; reporting to him is a general superintendent. Under the general superintendent are five department superintendents, each running a general area of the assembly line. Depending upon the extent and complexity of activities, each department superintendent has between one and four general foremen reporting to him. A general foreman might be in charge of one to six section foremen. Each section foreman has between fifteen and forty hourly wage employees under him. (When the plant is operating on a two-shift basis, the structure of organization below the level of department superintendent is duplicated.) In all, there are approximately 20 general foremen, just over 100 foremen, and between 2,000 to 5,000 production workers, depending upon the rate of production.

Approximately one third of the plant population is made up of persons in nonproduction groups. The title of the chief officers of each of these groups and the functions they head are as follows:

| Title | Group Functions |
|---|---|
| Resident Comptroller | General accounting, budgetary control, payrolls, internal audits, reporting of |

| | direct-indirect labor costs, efficiency reports, capital and other expenditures, accounts payable, accounts receivable, etc. |
|---|---|
| Personnel Director | Labor relations and personnel administration, wage and salary, medical, cafeteria, safety, suggestion system, recruitment, induction, employment, insurance, compensation, training, public relations, performance rating, plant protection, etc. |
| Plant Engineer | General plant maintenance, plant layout, equipment installation, physical maintenance and supplies, heat and power, construction, etc. |
| Director of Material and Production Control | Internal production schedules, supplying production departments with parts, materials, material schedules, stock handling and distribution, liaison with suppliers, etc. |
| Supervisor Work Standards | Time and motion studies, work performance evaluation, balancing manpower to line speed requirements, work simplification, enforcement of divisional work standard procedures and requirements, etc. |
| Chief Inspector | Inspection of materials at receiving points, during assembly process, and at final point of shipment; reporting of defective parts, materials, or workmanship; receiving and acting on reports from car divisions and dealers. |

The functions of the remaining three staff groups headed by the traffic manager, general supervisor of engineering specifications, and the car distributor are not crucial to the present inquiry; their functions are not related directly to the production organization.

Although the plant manager is held responsible for the final product, it should be noted that his actions and those of his subordinates are frequently circumscribed by policies, procedures, rules, orders, and reporting systems controlled at divisional and corporate levels. Thus, for example, certain functions of the comptroller cannot be changed by order of the plant manager; the corporation must insist on standardized reporting procedures on all matters of finance and accounting. Similarly, the plant manager cannot order the personnel director to alter basic corporation policies with respect to salary administration, pension programs, insurance, and many other items; the corporation-wide labor agreement binds each plant to specific procedures. Many decisions of interpretation are controlled at levels above those of the local personnel director or the plant manager. Plant Y and other final-assembly plants must conform to inspection requirements established not only by the division itself, but by other divisions which fabricate parts and materials for assembly at Plant Y. The plant manager does not have authority to make large capital expenditures until specifically authorized by the corporation through the division. In many other areas, the plant manager is limited in his actions because of policies deemed essential by the division or by the corporation.

Despite the several limitations on the plant manager's authority, the division and corporation, in their policy statements and in informal remarks to this researcher, placed considerable stress on the fact that the manager is "master in his own house." The corporation has long stated a policy of "decentralization of management." To quote a high official at corporation headquarters: "If the plant manager can consistently deliver the goods below a certain cost ceiling within an acceptable quality range, keep up his schedules, and not run afoul of corporation policy, then how he runs his own show is pretty much his own business."

It is worth repeating that from 1953 to 1956 there were almost no changes in the plant organization structure; the number of levels remained the same; no new departments were added, eliminated, or consolidated; written statements on corporate and divisional policies, in general, remained virtually unchanged; position descriptions that set forth the areas of authority and responsibility of each salaried position, were not changed; above the plant level, those occupying the key line positions in the chain of command, from division manager up through corporation president, were the same persons holding the same offices at both points in time.

## B. BASIC TECHNICAL SYSTEM IN BOTH TIME PERIODS [1]

Although the present study is concerned with the sociology of a complex organization, certain technical facts cannot be ignored. The physical geography, plant layout, tools, system of supply and scheduling, methods of assembly—all these influence and often determine the behavior of the organization's members.

In the total production flow Plant Y is the final operation in a series of highly synchronized operations which begin at the ore pits and coal mines and carry through into basic manufacturing and the fabrication of several thousand parts. At a prescribed moment in time and space, these thousands of parts and units are brought to a focal point—the final assembly plant. Here the many products of previous operations are fed into a maze of conveyors and machinery and emerge as completed automobiles at a rate of over 350 each eight-hour day, or well over 700 units on a two-shift basis.

The plant itself covers over twenty acres of floor space. The dominant feature of the assembly plant is the great conveyor that winds through the plant for a total length of over two and a half miles. Feeding into the main line are two miles of

---

[1] Parts of the following description are drawn from C. R. Walker, R. H. Guest, A. N. Turner, *The Foreman on the Assembly Line* (Cambridge, Mass.: Harvard University Press, 1957). Permission granted by authors and Harvard University Press.

overhead and auxiliary lines carrying small parts, materials, and unit assemblies to appropriate stations along the line. Off the main line at many points are subassembly operations; some are conveyors and some are stationary "bucks" or benches. Apart from the administration area, the plant itself is divided into two large sections, each fed by rail spurs. In one area, the materials are taken from railroad cars and distributed to the first department in the series of assembly operations. Here the raw parts, panels, doors, and so on, are welded together to form the metal body of the car. Transferred to another section of the conveyor known as the "paint department," the body undergoes a series of painting operations. Next the body is "dressed up" in the trim department. Fittings are installed, glass inserted, and molding, chrome trim, cloth linings, and instrument panels are put in place. The seats and seat backs, which have been made in a separate section of the plant, are conveyed in and installed.

After the body is polished and "fitted up," it moves to the second major plant area known as the "chassis department." While the car body has been going through the operations just described, the car chassis has started on its way. Frames, arriving by rail, have moved along a spring and axle assembly line. Engines, sent from an engine plant several hundred miles distant, are attached to the built-up frame, and the wheels are affixed. After many other operations, the chassis arrives at the final line, where the body specifically designated for a given chassis is lowered at the "body drop" and fastened to the chassis. Among the several operations which follow are the attachment of hoods, grilles, front fenders, bumpers, lights, and many more units. The completed automobile is then tested, adjusted, and given final conditioning in the last department, "car conditioning." From here the vehicle goes into temporary storage from which it is shipped on to the dealers.

A striking feature of the over-all operations at Plant Y is that many different types of cars are assembled. Three distinct "makes" of automobiles are turned out, each make in many models and styles. Each body is painted with one of 45 or more distinct colors, and these colors can be applied in more than 200 combinations. There are 200 separate accessory specifications, and in addition, the various models have different color combinations for instrument panels and upholstery. Thus, the combinations are, as one member of management put it, "astronomical." Schedules are so contrived as to permit any car with any variety of specifications to be preceded or followed by a car of a completely different type with different specifications.

Operations as complex as these in automobile assembly require an enormous amount of planning and co-ordination by specialized technical groups. In fact, the ratio of persons in production activities to those in service, control, or reporting positions is two and a half to one.

This study deals with a technical organization and a human organization both of which are highly complex. The whole labyrinth of men and machines is organized in accordance with relatively simple principles of mass production, or more accurately, principles of progressive assembly. These principles derive from the basic concepts of standardization, interchangeability, precision, synchronization, and continuity. The product must progress through the shop in a series of planned operations; the right part must arrive precisely in the right place at the right time. Parts are delivered mechanically to and from the individual operators. Operations are broken down into simple constituent components at the place of assembly.

A technical organization such as an assembly line is highly sensitive to any kind of change. A mechanical breakdown or an error in human communication can upset the work flow of the entire plant. A change in production schedule, and especially the annual model change, causes a realignment and a reshuffling of literally thousands of work elements. Each breakdown or change sets in motion a whole series of actions within the managerial organization from foreman to manager and higher. New activities stimulate new interactions of people in the several hierarchical groups and between members of the production and nonproduction groups. As one observes what goes on in a complex production organization such as this, it becomes increasingly apparent that the "social system" cannot be divorced from the "technological system"; the two systems are inseparable.

# CHAPTER 3

# Plant Y in 1953—The Period of Disintegration

The end of the Korean War found the automobile industry "going all out" to meet the demands of the market. Plant Y and some of its sister plants in Corporation X not only stepped up line speeds but began operations on a two-shift basis. Schedules had to be rearranged, hourly workers had to be recruited and trained, and large numbers of supervisory and staff people had to be placed on new jobs. Anyone acquainted with industrial operations can understand the kinds of stresses brought on by such conditions. Plant Y was no exception—nor were its sister plants. However, in the judgment of top corporate management Plant Y was failing to adjust to the new demands on output. In comparison with other plants, costs were too high and schedules were not being met properly. Something was obviously going wrong. Members of the Plant Y staff were acutely aware of the situation they faced. This section describes their reactions from manager through the foremen in the line organization and their perceptions of their relationship to those in other departments.

## A. VERTICAL RELATIONS IN THE PRODUCTION ORGANIZATION

### 1. The Manager's Relations to Superiors and Subordinates

The number of contacts between the division and the plant, particularly with the plant manager, had been increasing during late 1952 and early 1953. Most of the reported com-

munications originated at the division level and were directed
toward the manager in the form of demands for better performance. "Pressure" was the common expression used at all
levels. Urgent telephone calls, telegrams, letters, and memo-
randa were being received by the plant from central headquarters. Higher officials were making more frequent visits to Plant
Y than to any of the other plants. Divisional staff members
representing accounting, quality control, material control,
personnel, and other functions were in frequent touch with
their subordinate counterparts in the plant and with the
manager himself. Dealers of the product were complaining
about poor delivery dates and alleged quality defects. The car
divisions whose products were being assembled at Plant Y were
communicating almost every day with the manager and his
staff, either directly or through division officials.

Faced with an increase in directives from above and cogni-
zant of Plant Y's low performance position, the manager knew
that he was, as he put it, "on the spot." To his subordinates,
carrying out directives from the division manager appeared to
be his chief preoccupation. For example, on at least two occasions he made recordings of his staff meetings and played
them back to the division manager. As one official observed
later: "He was trying to show the division manager that he
was carrying out orders. I think he was also trying to put the
blame on his own staff. They knew this."

The manager himself explained to this observer his own
position during the crisis period:

> "They just don't know in the central office what we have to
> face. They don't know how to get down to our level. They think
> everything can be done by a schedule, no matter how fantastic.
> They keep saying to me, 'Why can't you do it? So-and-so in
> another plant can.' Then when so-and-so has the same problem,
> they shift to another so-and-so. This competition thing can be
> carried too far. When I get this kind of pressure on me, I've
> always been able to roll with the punches, but now I get butter-
> flies in my stomach. It makes it hard for me. I can't tell those
> below me that I can't do anything about this impossible schedule,

so of course I get blamed for a lot of it. I can't treat my superintendents the way I get treated. They would just pack up and go home.

"I can't say these things to my people. I can't say them to my superiors. Results are all that matter to them. I wish I had some way of getting this up to the top where it might do some good. It comes from the very top of the corporation. I would get hung if I said this higher up.

"We have a labor turnover right now hitting close to sixty men a day. Still they call me up from central headquarters and ask me why I'm not on schedule.

"The new men we got are no good. Just yesterday I jumped a man who was not on his job. I asked where he was going and if he had asked permission. It's impossible for me alone to keep everybody in line, but I do the best I can."

The manager's comments and those of others show a distinct pattern, as well as a curious inconsistency. To the manager the pattern of communications was characterized by the constant use of orders and threats by the division; the manager no longer felt he had the "power" to respond effectively; his role was primarily defensive. Unable to show results, he felt he had to prove that he was "putting the pressure" on his subordinates according to his perception of the division's expectations. He felt he was the victim of conditions—the "impossible" production schedule over which he had no control. The division policy of encouraging interplant competition, a policy generally accepted by the other plant managers, was not considered legitimate by this manager, at least in the way it was being used on him by the division.

The inconsistency in his comments is that he indicated reluctance to deal with subordinates the way the division was dealing with him, yet a few moments later he described how he "jumped a man" and tried "to keep everybody in line." He appeared to denounce interplant competition himself, but his subordinates accused him of encouraging the same kind of interpersonal and interdepartmental rivalry.

Division officials on several occasions had reported that com-

pany policy was to allow plants to run their own operations
with a minimum of direction from above. The role of the
division's staff was to assist the plants, not to direct their activities. The manager at Plant Y did not, at this time, look
upon his superiors' behavior as action designed to help him
achieve the company's production goals. Neither the division
head nor the manager felt that the other was carrying out the
expected role in achieving the common goal—profit for the
corporation.

## 2. *Subordinates' Relations to the Plant Manager*

What the manager had to say about the division was closely
paralleled by what superintendents, general foremen, and
others at Plant Y had to say about the manager. "He puts the
heat on us and we can't talk back," is the way one general foreman summed it up.

Two general types of contacts between the manager and
his subordinates were noted in addition to written directives:
those involving the manager and his staff as a group (set
events) and those involving the manager and single individuals
(paired events). The manager often called for meetings with
his staff, sometimes once a week. Most of these meetings were
not scheduled on a regular basis; they were called as a direct
result of some new directive or complaint from the division
or as a result of some emergency situation in the plant. In
content, the meetings focused on short-run solutions to immediate production problems. Few were directed at what the
members called "long-range planning." In the meetings, the
manager generally directed remarks to one or another individual; he would request information on a given problem or ask
for an explanation; he frequently interrupted the members,
they reported, with his own opinions or orders; there were
few lateral discussions among members of the staff. As a department head later observed:

"We spent most of our time making explanations about why
something went wrong and who made it go wrong. Each one
tried to cover up for his own department, trying to prove he was

carrying out orders like Mr. Stewart[1] [the manager] said we should. We all recognized that the squeeze was on the manager from above, but he didn't have to hammer away with orders to get this done or that done, when no single one of us could do much about it."

What the department head was saying, in effect, was that the manager's directives toward individuals largely ignored the group *as a group,* and that the plant's technical difficulties could not be solved by the isolated actions of the person representing one special function in the total organization.

Most events involving the manager and single members of the line organization assumed essentially the same pattern— that of giving orders and directives to individuals, regardless of the effects of such orders on other individuals or groups. The manager's frequent trips to the production departments were usually his direct response to an emergency condition, such as a line breakdown, a report of continued quality trouble, or a stoppage in the material flow to operating stations. The manager asked questions and gave direct orders. As one general foreman put it: "He has the first and last word. I just say 'yes, sir.'"

Expressed feelings about the manager's actions were almost entirely negative on the part of the respondents. Beginning with the department superintendent level, and continuing to the foreman level, the following are a few remarks that are not exceptions. In noting them, the reader might keep in mind the manager's expressed feelings about his own relationship to his divisional superiors: "They don't know how to get down to our own level."

*a) Superintendents' Relations to the Plant Manager*

Superintendents spoke about their relationship to the manager in this manner:

"When me or my foremen would see the manager coming in, we'd all run away because we knew what it meant—trouble."

---

[1] All names are fictitious.

"The foremen under me don't make any decisions. They're scared to. I've had my boss come to me and say, 'Get this done,' but he never suggested how it was to be done or asked me how I thought it should be done. So in front of him I have to go down and chew out my foreman and then the foreman chews out the men. That seems to satisfy my boss, and maybe the thing does get done, but there's a bad feeling all around. My boss can't be that bad a guy. He must have gotten it from the plant manager."

"This plant is a one-man show, so people are not taught to be self-reliant. Fear, that's the trouble. Nobody questions an order. If the boss said 'Break a window,' most of the fellows would do just that. In the meetings we have they just give us hell. Nothing constructive is ever done."

Notice how these superintendents, each responsible for the actions of three to six hundred subordinates, perceived the manager's behavior in much the same manner as the manager himself did when speaking about his superiors. They were motivated to act on orders not because they believed these orders would satisfy either their own needs or solve technical problems; their response to orders appeared to be based solely on the fear that their jobs were at stake.

*b) General Foremen's Relations to the Plant Manager*

At the next level down the line organization, general foremen perceived the manager's behavior in much the same way:

"The trouble with the manager is that he doesn't really know what the problems are out in the shop. There are a lot of little things the men and foremen are asking for that don't amount to a hill of beans, but his answer is 'No' all the time. He won't have any trouble if he just takes the time to listen to some of the gripes. You can't simply ignore them. After a while the little things build up into big things, and that's what has happened here."

"Everyone seems to think worse of everyone else. The plant operates in a constant atmosphere of suspicion and pressure. In other plants top management starts off with an initial good opinion of the average worker. Not here. No one tries to understand the other fellow's point of view. If you're going to do anything about a situation like this, you've got to start at the top. And I don't mean just words. I don't mean just talking about human relations the way they do in a training program. I mean actions, not words, are what count. I don't think you can ever change the way of life of so many people. That's what it is here—a way of life with supervision and management, and I don't see how it can be changed."

"The top people are too quick to condemn, and they never compliment the men for a good job. They tell us it is good human relations to do it, but they don't do it themselves. The only time I have anything to do with the manager is when he comes down and chews me out, usually in front of others. I expect to be called on the carpet for the mistakes I make, but this should be done by my own boss. The trouble with this plant is that those at the top are doing most of the chewing out directly. On the second shift I get less of this just from the simple fact that the top people are not around as much. But this is no way to run a plant. If you have an organization and it spells out who is to order who around, then they should use it. I go to the men directly but only to look at the workers' problem. I don't bawl them out."

"One of the reasons we are getting ourselves fouled up is because the top boss has the idea that the rules aren't being enforced strictly. He's a smart man and I give him credit for that, but this plant can't run on rules alone. Next week, for example, he has ordered that everyone has to work exactly from whistle to whistle. I don't look forward to enforcing the rule. It's been a custom for years to allow some wash-up time."

Although these general foremen were farther removed from the manager in the "chain of command" than were the superintendents their perception of the manager's behavior was hardly different from that of the department superintendents. Obedience to orders, enforcement of rules, the exercise of power through threat of punishment, failure to listen—these were the chief characteristics of the manager's behavior as seen by general foremen.

### c) Foremen's Relations to the Plant Manager

At the next and lowest level of the managerial organization, fewer comments specifically directed at the manager's behavior were made. The average foreman—there were over 100 of them—saw considerably less of the manager than did those at higher levels. The expressed feelings among those who did make some observations about the manager were entirely negative. Here are two typical comments:

> "There is no recognition of the foremen. Top management are just hypocrites. The manager goes around making speeches about 'humanics.' He stresses the three 'C's,' which mean 'centrally controlled co-operation.' It's centrally controlled all right, but it's not co-operation. Everybody cuts the other guy's throat. They tell you to stress quality, but if you don't get production, before you know it you're on the outside looking in."

> "The manager would come down and stand next to me and point out some man and say, 'What the hell is that guy doing?' I get all nervous and confused and I suppose I'm expected to do something about it. The man may have a perfectly good excuse, but I have to pretend to straighten it out then and there. That doesn't make it any easier for the foreman with his men. You can't work under a manager like that."

These comments by foremen are hardly different in substance from what general foremen and superintendents said about the manager and, indeed, what the manager said about his superiors.

### 3. *Superior/Subordinate Relations below the Plant Manager*

In a hierarchical organization it is axiomatic that information and orders are generally transmitted through the chain of command from superior to subordinate. It is assumed, also, that the upward flow of communications generally takes place in reverse through these same channels. Supervisors at middle and lower levels reported that the overwhelming number of contacts were initiated by superiors, that most contacts involved the issuance of orders by superiors, and that these communications took place in response to immediate technical and organizational emergencies.

The expressed feelings about relationships down the chain of command of the line organization can be arbitrarily separated into two categories: feelings of a subordinate to a superior and the reverse.

Comments of subordinates about superiors were generally negative, and they revealed varying degrees of antagonism and fear.

### a) General Foreman's and Foreman's Relations to Superiors

Below is one of several comments made by *general foremen* which illustrates the prevailing feelings which most subordinates held for superiors and the reasons that were behind these feelings:

> "Take like on this scheduling problem I'm having. The line today is all out of balance, and the heavy jobs are bunching through all at once. We can't keep to the schedule, and our quality is shot to hell. Some of us know what the trouble is, but does my boss or the fellows in the front office come down to get our opinion of what's wrong? Hell, no. The boss comes up to me today and throws a standard quality report in my face. So I have to do something. He outranks me, so I have to go through the motions of telling my foremen to straighten it out. The trouble here is that there is too much of this superiority in rank. This prevents people from getting right down to brass tacks and finding out what the real trouble is."

What this general foreman resented most was that he was being accused of failing to carry out an essential function, that is, seeing to it that the cars met quality standards when, as he saw it, the condition was beyond his immediate control. His frustration over this "technical" difficulty was deepened by the perceived actions of his superior. The superior in this instance used the impersonal mechanism of a quality report to force the general foreman to act. The general foreman considered this action paramount to an order which could not be questioned. Acting from fear, he felt obliged to tell his foreman to "straighten it out." Notice that the general foreman was willing only "to go through the motions" of telling his foreman. The implication is that his intention was not to discipline the foreman, since it was not the foreman's fault. Nevertheless, the general foreman's *intention* and the foreman's *reaction* were strikingly different. The foreman, in describing this same general foreman's behavior, said:

> "My boss is sharp and he knows how this scheduling business raises the devil in my section, but he is under a helluva lot of pressure. He's just as scared of his job as we are. He comes over and tells me to get my quality in better shape. It's one thing to issue an order; that's the easy way out. It's quite something else to carry it out when you can't control what causes the trouble."

Lack of time to exchange information, fear of the consequences of not obeying orders, and doubts about the legitimacy of orders were often cited as sources of friction between a subordinate and his boss. One general foreman described the situation this way:

> "Foremen now just don't have the proper time to spend with their men. They are scared, and they hide behind their authority, which is pretty shaky anyhow. They issue orders because they are told to. They often don't know what the orders are for. As a general foreman, I try to explain, but either I don't have the time, or I'm not convinced the orders are any good anyhow. My boss doesn't explain them to me very often."

Most of the *foremen,* after making generalized statements about their superiors' perceived behavior, such as, "It's misery and friction all the time," or "That pressure is crazy; it knocks you out," then elaborated on their feelings toward superiors. Two of the more typical comments were the following:

> "My general foreman is all strictly business. The only time I see him is when he comes down to bawl me out for something. That happened just a few minutes ago. I was scared to explain what the trouble was and to ask him to help me out."

> "The general foreman is the real boss of the men and not the foreman. Anything he says goes. The foreman has to take it, and he doesn't have anybody to go to. The men have a union, but the foreman can't turn anyplace."

This latter comment reflects the familiar "man-in-the-middle" aspect of the foreman's role. He is subject to punishment from above if he fails to carry out orders; if he carries out orders just as they are given, he runs the risk of alienating his men. His men have a mechanism of appeal through the union; the foreman feels he has none. The curious fact is that even those at higher levels in the organization expressed substantially the same feelings about not being able to appeal the actions of superiors. The plant manager himself, it is recalled, said, "I can't say these things to my people. I can't say them to my superiors."

As indicated earlier, it was not uncommon for members of higher levels in supervision to ignore the chain of command and to initiate contacts directly with those some levels below. As one superintendent observed:

"I came from another plant as department superintendent. First thing that struck me here was that they were not paying any attention to the line organization. There's too much of the superintendent giving orders directly to the foreman and by-passing the general foreman."

Foremen, more than any other group, often cited the effects of level skipping on themselves and on their subordinates. One of them said, characteristically:

"I get aggravated by the interference from the general foreman and the superintendent. They are always trying to run the men in my section. Today the general foreman stopped a man on the line and told him off. I heard about it later. This has happened before, and I've seen one of my men quit on the spot. I resent this. I feel I should have a chance to try things my way first. This interference weakens my position with the men. The men get to wonder who is their boss, and I don't blame them."

Failure to follow the chain of command was especially resented in matters involving rule infractions by subordinates. Top plant management in 1953 placed considerable stress on the rules as such, but in the judgment of middle and lower supervision, the manner in which rules were enforced often created difficulties far beyond those which the rules themselves were designed to eliminate.

Among the several standing rules were those related to absentees. Absenteeism had been increasing substantially. Upper management came to rely more and more on stricter rule enforcement. Moreover, final decisions on disciplinary measures were to an increasing extent being assumed by those at levels higher than the foreman. One superintendent observed:

"They've gone too far on this business of investigating workers who are absent. Piling up a lot of rules on top of each other and enforcing them is not going to solve what's wrong with us. I was ordered by the production manager yesterday to personally investigate two cases of hourly workers. This should be the foreman's job and not a department superintendent's. In one case, a man's wife had already called up the plant doctor, who had properly notified my foreman. But how do you think the man felt when I called later to find out why he was absent?"

A foreman in this same superintendent's department showed little awareness of the superintendent's feelings and simply "fixed the blame" on the superintendent:

"The superintendent goes strictly by the book on this business of absenteeism. If a man is out so many times, he should be fired. But the foreman often knows the circumstances. The foreman should have the final word about a man being absent so much."

What subordinates had to say about the actions of superiors closely paralleled what was said about the plant manager. All spoke as if the very existence of their jobs was at stake. Obedience to orders was an end in itself. Some subordinates believed that those at higher levels did not understand or even care to understand the technical and administrative problems which subordinates faced. Others thought that superiors were aware of the problems but felt helpless to do anything about them.

How, then, did superiors look at their subordinates' behavior? Here one finds that the plant manager's observations about his subordinates are repeated in superior-to-subordinate observations down the line. The manager, it may be recalled, expressed a reluctance to deal with subordinates "the way I get treated [by the division]." Yet a few sentences later he defended the necessity of "jumping on a man who was not on his job." It was later pointed out that subordinates perceived little or no "sympathy" on the manager's part. Many were aware of the pressures he was under, but they judged him primarily on the basis of his actions toward them.

These same inconsistencies were observed in what the superintendents and general foremen said. A superintendent, a few minutes after stating that "a little decent treatment can be quickly absorbed by the men and the people below me," insisted that many of his foremen "had to be jumped on to keep them in line." Most of the general foremen expressed concern about the reaction of their foremen to the extreme pressures they were under, yet often admitted that emergencies of the moment left them with no alternative but to step in and arbitrarily issue orders. One of them, for example, expressed this same concern but later, during a discussion on the shop floor, observed:

> "Take that foreman right over there. He complained to me that a man was too tall for the job. I told him he wasn't, and I told him further that he wasn't to make such moves without consulting me."

The same foremen referred to by the general foreman described the same incident:

> "Just yesterday my general foreman bawled the hell out of me because I did not want to put a big man on a cramped-up job inside the car body. It didn't make sense."

Only one among the eight general foremen interviewed expressed no concern about his superior's behavior toward him nor about the effects of his actions on subordinates. To him the use of raw disciplinary power was normal and effective. In short, he wholly accepted "the system." As he described one type of action:

> "These headliners [a group of workers on one section of the line] stick together. It's awfully difficult to 'get' a man for doing something wrong. The trouble with the foremen, especially the new ones, is that they are too sympathetic with the men. What I do when I catch a man is to pull the job off the line, then rub

his nose in it. I tell him, 'If you don't like it, why don't you get out?' That usually works."

The feelings which foremen expressed (in the interview) toward their immediate workers showed the same kind of ambivalence which those at higher levels had expressed. They condemned their superiors' behavior toward them. They disliked having to "deal with" their workers in the same way, but they admitted that under the circumstances they often had to behave this way. It was part of the system. One of them said: "I have two choices: put the squeeze on my men or get out. I don't like either one." Another said:

> "I hate to yell at my men, but sometimes I'm forced to do it. You can't be a good foreman at the same time you're scared. It's not just the foremen; some department heads yell at us and at the men. Maybe it's because they are getting it from *their* bosses, but I don't think they should pass it on like that."

The dilemma of how a supervisor wanted to behave toward subordinates and how he felt he had to behave was in many instances more sharply and vigorously expressed by the newer foremen. Many of these persons had recently been promoted from the ranks. They continued to accept, for a while at least, norms of behavior which hourly workers thought were legitimate. A remark made by one of the foremen reveals the transition which took place when he became a foreman. As he put it:

> "When I used to be a man on the line, I knew the way I'd like to be treated. When I got to be foreman, I started to treat my men in the same way . . . but you just can't do that. You can't change overnight what's been going on for fifteen years. Now I treat my men the way they have been treated more or less in the past. If a man is habitually late . . . I just turn him in, that's all. They can always quit if they don't like the job."

(It might be observed that statements such as: "If you don't like it, etc.," were repeated more frequently by hourly employees in describing management's behavior toward them than any other single expression from the 218 interviews.)

## B. *RELATION OF PRODUCTION TO NON-PRODUCTION GROUPS*

All large-scale industrial organizations have departments whose functions are not related directly to the making of the product. Some of the functions are established to give direct *service* to production; some act as *control;* some serve only in a *reporting* capacity. These departments and their formal functions at Plant Y have already been described. They include accounting, personnel, plant maintenance, material and production control, work standards, inspection, and others. While each has a primary service, control, or reporting function, a particular department may often act in two or three capacities.

Progressive assembly operations require close co-ordination between the activities of the operating (line) groups and those of the nonproduction departments. To members of operating supervision, this co-ordination was particularly important with respect to material and production control and to inspection.

### 1. *Material and Production Control*

Each station and each section of the assembly line requires materials and parts to "flow" in adequate quantity to the right place at the right time in accordance with the established line schedule. Any failure on the part of the service department responsible for the flow of materials may result in production difficulties, even to the extent of shutting down the conveyor.

Bottlenecks and shortages were chronic in the 1953 period. In some respects the problem was a technical matter; the system of material flow and the layout of equipment was inadequate in some areas. As the technical difficulties worsened, interpersonal conflicts increased. These conflicts in turn created further technical difficulties.

In each operating section under a foreman there was a representative of the material department, commonly known as a "stock chaser." His job was to expedite delivery of the parts to be assembled to the section. When operators on the line saw they were "running short," they would notify the stock chaser. In many sections, the stock chaser was unable to follow through on all requests because there were so many of them. The foreman was also notified by the operator or by the stock chaser. He would then act as a stock chaser himself and look for materials. Often he was unable to seek out the sources of the holdup, so he informed the general foreman. The general foreman in turn would request action from a supervisor in the material department. Often the general foreman was unable to follow through immediately on all of the recurring requests from his foremen. The general foreman would call or leave a message with the department superintendent.

A similar sequence of communication took place up the chain of command beginning with the material department itself. Those on the top, the production manager or plant manager, would hear of the difficulty either from a subordinate in the production department or from someone in the material department. The action which followed was usually a direct order for one or the other groups "to straighten out the mess." Often orders were issued by someone at a high level directly to those at the lowest levels.

In content, most contacts were made in response to problems requiring an immediate solution. There were very few instances in which two persons, one from production and one from the material department, held long discussions or a series of discussions over time for the purpose of agreeing on long-range solutions. This was true at all levels. Moreover, when specific directives were issued from higher authorities, there was little evidence to indicate that other departments, whose functions were closely linked to both production and materials, had a "say" in the decision itself. Any decision, either by a production supervisor or by a member of the material department, was likely to affect the routine of other service, control, and reporting groups such as work standards, maintenance, and inspection.

In one sense, communications between the production department and other departments, such as the material department, were similar to what might be expected from the formal organization chart. The chart shows no links between departments at lower levels. This formal separation of function and lack of communications between the production and material groups were sources of frequent complaints. One superintendent, for example, made the following observations:

> "The line and service departments never get together to decide on a policy. If the material department wants to do something, they run to the front office, get backing from the top, and then they cram it down your throat. We do the best we can, but the next thing we know someone higher up comes down and threatens: 'If you can't do it that way, we'll get somebody in here who can.'"

A general foreman, looking back in 1956 at the 1953 conditions, made a similar point:

> "The common expression here was, 'This is how we're going to lay out our material control; now you make it work.' I'm afraid this was the plant manager's attitude, but it did more harm than good because what was effective from the material point of view was not necessarily good from a production point of view."

Another general foreman described a typical sequence of events stemming from a material holdup:

> "Take on this business of not getting the right materials on the line at the right time. A line like this depends upon good material flow. A shortage holds up the operator. The foreman asks the operator 'Why the holdup?' The foreman comes to me about it. I call the material department. First time they ever heard about it. Say they'll check. Nothing happens. I go look for myself. My foreman in the meantime is getting into other troubles, and I'm not around to help."

The recurring theme in interviews with those most directly affected by actual or threatened material shortages—the foremen—was that large segments of their time were taken up "chasing down shortages" which took them away from other supervisory duties.

## 2. *Inspection*

Closely linked to the activities of the production groups were those of inspection. In most sections of the line, there were inspection check points. These check points were manned by inspectors who were ultimately responsible to the chief inspector, not to the section foreman or to other production supervisors. This sharp separation of function is characteristic of many industrial plants and is based on the rational principle that those primarily responsible for *quantity* of production should not be in a position to pass on the *quality* of their products.

At the foreman-inspector level, the following communications pattern prevailed throughout all sections of Plant Y in the 1953 period. Inspectors marked faulty work for repairs. Sometimes they notified the foreman, sometimes the repairman. Often inspectors were urged to report trouble only to their direct superior (the inspection foreman). The inspection foreman would notify the production foreman, who in turn would check on or admonish the worker.

Standard quality reports took a longer route. These would be routed through the inspection organization to top plant management. Inquiries and directives would then be issued down the line of the production organization.

In inspection/production relationships, a pattern was observed which paralleled that of material/production relationships. Lateral communications were limited to accusations and defenses, with either one party or the other at any given level making a point and not engaging in sustained discussions as to the long-range solution of a given quality problem. The general tendency was for each to have the problem solved by submitting the matter to higher authority through channels.

Foremen fully accepted the necessity for having inspection kept strictly separate from production. They accepted the fact that in any kind of industrial organization there were bound to be certain conflicts between the pressure of quantity and the pressure of quality. In this case they felt that the "principle" had been carried too far. What should have been merely a "technical" separation of function had become a bitter "personal" fight with inspection personnel. Whether justified or not they usually fixed the blame on the plant manager who, as they perceived his actions and directives, openly encouraged an extreme form of rivalry between the two groups.

A former inspection foreman described a sequence of events involving himself and production supervision:

> "I remember one time getting called on the carpet by the plant manager, and he told me, 'If you're afraid of the production people, then you're not a good inspection foreman. If you don't like the way it's going, then you just stop the line. If you can't do that, then you're not an inspector. Never be afraid of the production people.' The manager ordered me to have the maintenance department install a series of buttons throughout the shop, and he told me that any time I didn't like something to just go over and push the button and stop the line. Well, I had the buttons installed all right, but I never used them. I thought it would do more harm than good. After all, I have to live with those production people every day."

This comment illustrated the dilemma in which members of Plant Y often found themselves—that of carrying out orders or enforcing rules which they did not consider "legitimate." This inspection foreman carried out the "letter" of an order from a superior. He had the buttons installed and could thus demonstrate, if called upon, that he had followed orders, but he was under still a different source of pressure from those he had to "live with." He knew that production supervisors could use informal but effective measures of retribution against him. He therefore made a compromise by installing the buttons, then not using them.

The "separation of powers" between inspection and production supervisors was constantly being stressed by higher management. Most supervisors expressed the need to be in close touch with inspection in order to gain a fuller understanding of quality requirements, but, as one department superintendent put it:

"The inspection and production people are too far apart. The chief inspector gets suspicious when he sees an inspector and foreman talking together. It seems like this is the attitude of top management in this plant . . . suspicion. I don't want to be that way. It's against the way I worked in another plant, but I feel like I'm being driven to be just the same way."

Many members of production supervision complained that the inspection department itself was not consistent in its judgment. They felt that line inspectors were allowing certain "jobs" to pass or not pass, but that final inspectors were using different standards. This only confused and antagonized the foremen. A general foreman described with considerable feeling the effects of this condition:

"The trouble with inspection is that what goes on with my inspectors may not 'go' with the final inspectors in car conditioning. It's more a matter of getting people together than anything else. The inspector should have an understanding with the foremen so that the foremen know exactly what inspection is looking for. Now it's just a fight between foremen and inspection foremen, with both fighting final inspection. When it becomes a personal fight between people as it is now, we lose sight of what we're trying to accomplish, and then we're sunk."

The implication of what this general foreman was saying is clear. He saw the need for a greater exchange of factual information between agents of the production and inspection departments. The information was in itself impersonal in that it was related to inspection standards of physical material, the product itself. Yet the continued misunderstanding led to "a personal fight between people," which in turn made it still more difficult to exchange the required technical information on matters of quality.

Foremen often observed the way in which misunderstandings about technical information led to interpersonal conflict, and which in turn prevented further exchange of technical information. This "snowballing" effect is described by one of the foremen as follows:

"Too often inspection gives us the sheets and leaves it up to the foreman just how to interpret the 'specs.' What happens so often is that a foreman would interpret them one way and the inspector another, and then maybe later another inspector at the end of the line interprets them still a different way. This just makes for a lot of squabbling."

The same feelings were expressed toward control functions other than inspection. The work standards department, in the foreman's judgment, "dictated" precisely how a foreman should distribute the work load of his hourly workers without getting the foreman's opinion. The accounting department issued general reports telling the foreman that his efficiency was poor without giving him specific information as to where and why. The production scheduling group changed schedules without due consideration of the current manpower situation.

Telling a foreman that his quality was poor, that his efficiency was low, and that his manpower was "out of line" did nothing, he thought, to help him solve his day-to-day operating problems. Those at higher levels often, in effect, agreed with the foremen's complaints but said they were powerless to do much. They were so preoccupied "putting out fires" there was no time for planning or for long-range preventive measures.

## C. *PLANT Y: PERFORMANCE–1953*

The description thus far of "what went on" at Plant Y in 1953 has been largely "qualitative"; the respondents described their relations to others as they saw the situation. It remains to look at behavior in terms of "quantitative" results. How well or how poorly did this organization perform? How did its performance in this period compare with the performance of five other plants producing precisely the same type of products?

The answers are found in management's own records of performance. Among the several indices seven are generally held to be most significant. These include: efficiency (direct costs), quality, indirect costs, safety, labor grievances, absenteeism, and turnover.

Plant Y's comparative record is as follows:

### 1. *Efficiency*

In 1953, Plant Y's efficiency was the poorest among the six plants of the division; it was utilizing 16 per cent more direct labor personnel than were called for by division-wide standards. (The next poorest performer in the division was only 10 per cent away from standard.)

### 2. *Quality Performance*

Based on records of dealer complaints, inspection checks from fabricating divisions, and internal final inspection counts, Plant Y was not only exceeding the maximum standard of defects and rejections set by the division, but it had the poorest quality record among all six plants.

### 3. *Indirect Labor Performance*

Costs of operating the material, maintenance, inspection, and other nonproduction departments were considerably higher than they were in any other plant in the division.

### 4. *Safety Record*

Plant Y alternated between last and next-to-last place in the division in the ratio of its monthly lost time accidents per 100 employees; it consistently held a position in the lowest quarter of all 126 plants of the corporation.

### 5. *Labor Grievances*

The average number of formal grievances per 100 employees was substantially higher at Plant Y than it was at all but one of the other plants in the division.

### 6. *Absenteeism*

Plant Y's monthly rate of absenteeism was substantially higher than that of the other plants in the division; it rarely fell below 4 per cent.

### 7. *Turnover*

The average monthly rate of quits and discharges was 6 per cent; in numbers it sometimes ran from 300 to 400 per month; this was double the turnover rate recorded for the average of the other five plants.

The consistently poor performance of Plant Y, when compared with the performance of other similar plants in the division, can hardly be accounted for by chance. Nor is there any evidence to indicate that the poor record of performance was a function of the plant's geographical location or of economic and market conditions which would affect it alone and not the other plants.

# CHAPTER 4

# Plant Y from 1953 to 1956

## A. *THE SUCCESSION OF A NEW PLANT MANAGER*

In the fall of 1953, the executives at the division and corporation levels decided to do something about what was frequently referred to in central headquarters as "a hopeless situation" at Plant Y. An unofficial and costly walkout in July, perhaps more than any other event, brought the matter to a head. To the top executives, the decision was based upon two simple facts: the cost of operating Plant Y was far higher than in any other plant in the division and quality of performance was poorer. Several explanations of Plant Y's problem were given to this observer at the time.

The division manager in charge of the several assembly plants took the position that, in addition to the failure of the plant manager, there were several supervisors in line and service departments who were "incompetent." The vice-president in charge of this particular division, as well as several other divisions, felt that a new man with "strong leadership traits" could "straighten the situation out." The executive vice-president in charge of all operations had the authority to make the final decision. He stated:

"Some members of top management have been telling me that because of the history of Plant Y there is not much that can be done. I have been told that most of the supervision is no good and that the workers are merely sitting down on the job. In my opinion, there is a lot more in the Plant Y situation than the quality of those in supervisory positions. Supervision has lost a lot of its enthusiasm, and in some ways you can't blame them. I think both supervision and the workers have some real complaints, and it is going to take a manager who can dig in and find out what is the matter. I used to be head of the war division at Plant Y and got to know quite a few people, and the people there are just as good as they are any place in the corporation. What they need is the chance to show their stuff. If we can spark it off with the right man and give him the right kind of support, there is no reason why Plant Y won't pull out of it."

After intensive discussion at corporate headquarters, the decision was made to replace the manager with Matthew Cooley, the production manager at one of the other plants. Cooley had been given considerable latitude in running production operations at Plant A and had demonstrated his ability to increase efficiencies. On short notice he was told to report immediately to Plant Y for assignment as plant manager. George Stewart resigned as manager with an early pension retirement arrangement.

When Cooley arrived at Plant Y accompanied by the division manager, an introductory dinner meeting was held in a hotel near the plant. The meeting was attended by all members of the managerial organization down through the foremen. As one of the general foremen described it a week after the meeting:

"When I went to this dinner meeting, the first thing that struck me was the way they had the seating arrangement. I think it was done very well. Whoever arranged it made sure that the old cliques they had in supervision were broken up. We also noticed that the new plant manager sat down among the foremen and general foremen. The vice-president [actually, the division manager] of the division introduced us to the new manager. The vice-president said something about his confidence in the new manager. We can remember when an earlier manager came here, and he got rid of a whole lot of people in supervision. He just gave them their walking papers and sent them on their way. We wondered what the new man was going to do."

This same general foreman then went on to point out that:

> "We expected that the new plant manager would probably hang around the division manager after the meeting was over. Big shots usually stick together, but he didn't. He just kept circulating on the floor and meeting as many of the guys as he could. I was quite surprised, and so were the others."

The new plant manager later stated to this observer that he received very few specific instructions from the division and corporation as to how to proceed. Cooley was assured by the division manager that he would have the "full backing of the division and the corporation in making Plant Y successful." He was told that he could have whatever personnel he needed. For a long time he had heard that "bad habits" had developed over the years, and that there were many people in the supervisory group and the work force who would never change. He had also been told that the best thing he could do was to "clear out the dead wood."

His first few days at the plant were spent getting acquainted with his staff and "sounding them out" on problem areas. In the first meeting with all supervision he put forward what he called "a few basic goals" for the organization in terms of expected efficiency and quality. He stated candidly to the group that Plant Y had a bad reputation. He said he had heard that many members of the group were not capable of doing their jobs. He said he was "willing to prove that this was not so, and until shown otherwise, I personally have full confidence in the group." He went on to say that his job was "not to catch and punish people for doing a poor job, but rather to help them in any way [he] could to do a good job." He also stated, "I don't believe in firing a lot of people and using threats and fear."

One of the first steps taken by the new manager was to send a letter to each foreman asking to be invited by the foreman to visit the foreman's section. The foremen indicated some surprise, and one of them said: "I guess this new fellow is a pretty good manager. He wants to be invited to come down to inspect my section. I'll be very happy if he does come around."

Also, within the first three days, Cooley met with the union shop committee, and after stating a few general objectives, urged them to make any comments they wanted to.

The union president reported the meeting this way:

"Cooley was introduced to all of us at a shop committee meeting. He told the committee in straight language just what he believed in and what he hoped to do at Plant Y. He said that before he came in he had been briefed on this plant, and that he had heard it was a lousy plant with lousy people in it, and that he was going to have to cope with this. Then he said that he didn't believe the story one single bit—that in the couple of days he had been around he had found that the people at Plant Y were okay. He said he was going to operate that way. Then he said that it was not his intention to negotiate on grievances, but that he was inviting us personally to see him any time about ways to make the plant better. He said he welcomed any suggestions.

"This was a completely new approach to the committee, and although some of the boys were skeptical, most of us felt that this man meant what he said. What a change!"

During the introductory period, it became evident to the manager in talks with his immediate staff, operating supervision, union committeemen, and hourly workers, and in his observations of the physical plant itself, that the organization was, as he put it, "operating from day to day on a kind of 'emergency' basis." Except for a certain amount of over-all planning at the corporation and division levels, there appeared to be little long-range planning at the local level. He said he recognized that the "co-operate-or-else" philosophy under which the plant had operated previously was not working. He added:

"I saw that the organization needed a long-range program spelled out in writing and reviewed with the department heads, the staff, and superintendents. They needed to be in agreement on something that was realizable and tangible and practical. It had to come from the whole organization and be explained to the whole organization, and for that portion of it which affects the hourly people, the union should be taken into confidence and be told what the long-range objectives would be from the point of view of their membership. Then we had to start moving on it."

The manager later observed, "As planning actually became an accomplishment, they began to trust you and build up mutual trust again."

One of the first steps taken by the manager was to get permission from the division to begin reduction of the long overtime hours. As a union officer put it:

"We have had managers come in and give us a lot of soft talk, but they never backed it up. This fellow showed up, and one of the first things he did was to cut down on the long hours which had been going on for months. It had been ragged on the men. I don't know how much the men realized who was responsible, but the committeemen knew it, and they must have passed it on. The average worker, I think, gets a lot of his impressions of management from the committeemen."

In the first few weeks under the new manager, no measurable changes in performance were noted. Indeed, it was to be many months before any results as measured by management's own standards would become apparent. Nevertheless, the behavior of the man occupying the formal office of manager evoked a considerable amount of favorable comment. In his public statements and in comments to individuals, he had dismissed the idea of a "wholesale housecleaning." He had said, in effect, that the organization could solve its own problems without the use of formal disciplinary powers from the top. Although he set forth a few general goals, the greater part of his time in the first few weeks was spent in observing technical operations and in listening to what others had to say.

## B. *THE INTRODUCTION OF MEETINGS*

During the months following Cooley's succession to office, he established a series of regularly scheduled meetings which in time directly or indirectly involved members of supervision at all levels. These continued for the balance of the new manager's term of office. The fact that men occupying different positions and charged with certain responsibilities were brought together in groups was not in itself a new phenomenon at Plant Y. The previous manager had often called his staff together as a group, but as was noted earlier, group meetings were usually called as a result of a current emergency; they were not scheduled regularly, the manager dominated the discussion, and the members looked upon them primarily as punitive sessions.

The scope and function of the meetings established by the new manager stood in marked contrast to those of the earlier period: there were more of them, they were regularly scheduled, they covered a wider range of activities, more people took part in them, and they were oriented not only to the present but to the immediate and long-range future.

The most general type of meeting was held once every month in the plant cafeteria and attended by all members of plant supervision. Its essential purpose, according to the manager, was "to tell everyone in the organization what was ahead for the next thirty days, review the past thirty days, and answer questions that come up." Supervisors were encouraged to submit written questions about any subject. The manager promised frank answers.

Once each week a meeting was held which included the manager and those reporting directly to him—his immediate staff. These meetings were concerned with new developments, information, and directives stemming from the division and corporation. Chaired by the plant manager, this group in time became a decision-making body for the plant as a whole.

Also once each week, a cost meeting was held by the comptroller and production manager with the plant manager present. Included were the heads of the personnel and work standards departments and all supervisors in the production organization down through the level of general foreman. The comptroller presented the current figures on costs and plant efficiency; the production manager made comments interpreting these figures. Questions and suggestions were put forward by the participants.

This same group, with the addition of the chief inspector,

met once a week to review matters relating to inspection and quality.

The director of material control met once a week with all of his salaried employees, including material control clerks. These meetings were often followed by sessions with the hourly wage stock handlers.

Within four months it was observed that operating and service departments at lower levels were also beginning to meet together. There is no indication that these meetings were specifically ordered by the plant manager or his immediate subordinates. One superintendent, for example, stated:

> "We get together a lot more in conference between me, the general foremen, and the foremen. When I was foreman, I would have given my right arm to have been able to sit down with the superintendent and feel free to discuss things and make suggestions. These meetings I have are nothing you might call formal. They are informal, and they cover all kinds of things that aren't scheduled at a certain time. We never had them before."

A general foreman three years later recalled how the early meetings with his group of foremen triggered new activities:

> "When things started a couple of years ago, I sat down with my foremen and we talked about things that should be done. Everybody knew what our problems were. It went right up to the division manager, but somehow we got the green light to go ahead and do something. At first I worked out my own program with my people and later it became part of a regular system. People knew what they were supposed to do, they knew what others were doing, and they could look ahead in the future a little bit."

Other general foremen made similar observations. These "get-togethers" were begun spontaneously by supervision without having been ordered from above. They were "group" activities of the sort which had not existed before. Reference to the "green light to do something" indicated that the fear complex was disappearing and that those at lower levels felt that the "higher-ups" would support greater self-determination of action at lower levels. The "program" was indigenous to the group and later "became part of a regular system." Cognition of how the action of one group fit into the functioning of the larger system was increasing. Finally (and this theme was expressed more often than any other), the meetings allowed the members to analyze current problems in order to lay out programs for future action.

It should be pointed out that several members of supervision at first thought that group meetings were too "time-consuming." "But," as a general foreman put it, "it began to dawn on us that if we ever were to stop running around and putting out fires, we had to do this. *Also, just getting together as a group was worth something in itself.*"

## C. SHIFTS IN PERSONNEL

When Cooley took over as plant manager in late 1953 he was told by his superiors that a "shake-up" in personnel at Plant Y was in order. The implication was clear that many supervisors "had to go," and that they were to be replaced by men from other plants in the division. Cooley was assured that he would be granted a free hand in drawing from other divisional personnel "to fill in the weak spots."

The new manager apparently chose not to follow the recommendations of higher officials—namely, "a wholesale housecleaning." Not long after succeeding to office, he did bring in a new production manager; another plant had requested the former production manager. Several foremen, general foremen, and three superintendents who were on temporary assignment at Plant Y returned to their "home" plants during the first year. They were not replaced by "outsiders"; their jobs were filled by persons within Plant Y itself.

During the first year and in the succeeding two years, Plant Y experienced many shifts in supervisory personnel. The records reveal that, between Cooley's arrival in September 1953 and May 1956, only 25 per cent of Plant Y's supervisors held the same job assignment throughout the period. To the line and staff supervisors themselves the most arresting fact about the changes was that, following Cooley's succession to office, *no more than three of the three hundred salaried personnel were discharged or asked to resign.* Many supervisors contrasted this fact with the earlier period when, according to their own estimates, between twenty-five and sixty supervisors had been summarily discharged from their jobs or demoted within one year.

The shifts in job assignments took many forms. An inspection foreman, for example, was transferred to the material control department and later was placed in charge of inspection for the entire plant. A foreman on the shipping line became number-two man in material control. A production foreman in the metal department was moved over to the chassis department, where he later became shift superintendent, then department superintendent. A young time study man, who in 1950 held a nonsupervisory position in the work standards department, was moved up rapidly, and by 1956 at the age of twenty-nine became production manager for the entire plant. The man he replaced was made plant manager at another plant.

The promotions were made possible for two reasons: (1) the vacancies that occurred when several members of supervision returned to their "home" plants, and (2) the vacancies that occurred when other plants requested some supervisors from plant Y. (In this latter connection, Plant Y in time came to be looked upon as a "training ground" for other plants.)

At the urging of the plant manager and through the vehicle of staff meetings, every supervisor in the organization was encouraged to develop understudies. The need for this became apparent as changes actually took place. A deliberate long-range program was instituted in which each member of management above the foreman level in the line and service departments gave his job over to one or more of his subordinates for a temporary period of sixty days.

As members of supervision often pointed out, in former times a supervisor had been reluctant to "build up" one of his subordinates. "The supervisor might find himself out of a job the next day."

Most of the personnel shifts which took place between 1953 and 1956 were not promotions but were lateral transfers to jobs on the same salary level. These transfers were not made as a result of some emergency; they were deliberate; they were planned. The largest single group of those transferred were production foremen.

The immediate effect of any given transfer from one section to another was that it took some time for the men transferred to become familiar with the new operations and a new group of subordinates. The long-run effects broadened his knowledge of the operations. As one foreman observed:

"The thing we have noticed is that they do move the foremen around a lot more than they ever did before. I think it is helpful because *it gives the foreman a much broader knowledge of the job.* Before, we used to scream at each other like a bunch of washerwomen, and that was mostly out of ignorance. Now, when some of the foremen go into some of the sections where they were before, they have a better appreciation of what their old problem was like."

Transfers were not made in large numbers at one time. The method was to pinpoint specific areas in order of priority and to "try out" a man for a period of time. If he did not "work out," he was not discharged but returned to the job he knew better. The plant manager described what he called his "method of attack":

"The chassis department was having the most trouble. The whole atmosphere and operating philosophy of everybody was, you might say, the fear complex. There just didn't seem to be any incentive to work. The superintendent originally said that the situation was hopeless and that the only solution he saw was that everybody should be fired. I don't think he meant everybody, but it showed how discouraging things were. What we did was to move two foremen and a general foreman from the metal department over to the chassis department. The metal department looked like the strongest department. We figured that a move like this might be one of the quickest ways to help the chassis department."

Shifts similar to this were made in other operating and service departments in later months.

## D. *CHANGES IN THE TECHNICAL ORGANIZATION*

Shortly after the succession of a new manager in 1953, there began a series of physical changes at Plant Y, which by 1956 had measurably influenced its performance. This study is not concerned with the physical improvements as such but with the interrelationship between the "technical" and "social" aspects of organization—a kind of interdependent phenomenon sometimes overlooked by those who study the dynamics of group behavior.

Plant Y was one of the oldest among all of the assembly plants in the division. Few major installations or changes in plant layout had been made for several years. It was corporation policy for all its plants and divisions to grant funds where there was a proven need and where there was reasonable assurance that the improvements would "pay off." Proof of need and assurance of economic justification rested primarily with the plant manager.

There is no indication that either Cooley or his new production manager came to Plant Y with any specific schemes for improving the physical plant. The manager's role in the first few months, as he saw it, was to ask questions and to find out what ideas for improvement would emerge from the group as a whole. The process of information gathering took several forms, the principal one being face-to-face conversations between the manager and his subordinates, supervisors on the lower level, hourly workers, and union representatives. Ideas were then listed for the agenda of the weekly planning sessions.

The first requests made to the division for capital expenditures were not concerned with increasing the efficiency of the line operations. In the manager's judgment, which was supported by his staff, the crucial need was to improve general working conditions for the hourly workers.

The cafeteria, for example, was poorly lighted, poorly ventilated, and "furnished with old wire ice cream parlor chairs with paper seats and tables which were obsolete." Funds were appropriated to refurnish it and to install new lights and air conditioning. New clothes lockers were installed in areas more convenient to the men. Parking areas were extremely crowded, and money was spent to expand new areas, including part of the lawn of the administration building. In certain sections of the plant, exhaust fumes were considered bad, and a number of exhaust fans were installed. Large heaters were brought in to compensate for cold drafts at the rail freight doors. Electric fans were installed in the areas that were particularly hot in the summer. The entire receiving area was relocated to eliminate the cold drafts and to facilitate more rapid unloading. Elevator platforms were put in to eliminate hand loading. The plant hospital was air conditioned. The washrooms were repainted and then later tiled. New plumbing was installed.

A union officer commented on some of these changes as follows:

"Cooley, just after he came in, went right to work to clean up the cafeteria and make something of it. It was in terrible shape, and it cost $15,000 to fix it up, but we could see that he meant business. And he fixed up the toilets in the paint shop. This didn't make much impression on the men, and they still didn't take care of them, but management kept fixing them up. The other manager simply said that the company would not fix them up. Cooley kept asking the union all the time for suggestions as to how they could be kept clean. He would always drop in on our committee meetings to get suggestions on these changes or to tell us first thing when he heard word that requests were approved. He did this on all the big plans or changes in policy."

While plans for improving the physical working conditions were being drawn up and put into effect, the organization was laying the groundwork for major changes and installations, the purpose of which was to improve the operations themselves. Work had already begun under the previous management on rebuilding the paint department. As the manager put it: "We ripped out the old ovens and put them on the roof. New spray booths were installed. We eliminated a lot of extra trucking. It helped on the fumes and the heat."

The next major physical changes were made in the metal

department. The metal finish section had become crowded and, hence, "uneconomical to operate." Storage facilities and conveyors were rearranged to allow more room. New lighting arrangements were made. The grinding booth, especially crowded, was doubled in length. The largest major layout rearrangement took place in what was known as the "trim department." The steady increase of additional car trim over the years had made the old layout unwieldly and overcrowded. The manager put it this way: "It wasn't only uneconomical, but it was a source of irritation for the workers and the foremen. Everybody was falling over everyone else."

This same kind of comment was repeated by almost every member of supervision whose section or department underwent physical changes. In looking back at former conditions they saw that interpersonal conflicts had often been generated by a technically inefficient layout and work flow. They saw these conflicts sharply reduced when the technical "bottlenecks" were eliminated.

The sequence of events leading to the physical changes is illustrated by the remarks of one of the general foremen. He described how the plant manager and production manager had first come around and asked foremen and general foremen for suggestions on how operations in the trim department could be improved. Later, according to the general foreman, his superintendent began to hold meetings with foremen and general foremen to discuss and agree upon a minimum number of changes. Next, the production manager took over a further series of meetings, which included members of the service as well as production groups. As the general foreman observed:

> "The material people and us had our differences of opinion but we thrashed it all out, and there was a good spirit about it. We finally arrived at something to satisfy all of us. We felt that they must have meant business this time because the okay came from the plant manager, if not higher."

The same pattern of action could be observed in the physical changes made in other sections of the plant. A superintendent described what took place in his department as follows:

"When Mat [the manager] first came around and talked with me, he told me outright that I couldn't possibly operate my department all crowded the way it was. This was welcome news to my ears, and I agreed with him one hundred per cent. Next thing we knew we were sitting down with the material department and plant engineers, the methods people and others and got together in some real give-and-take sessions and straightened out some of the material-handling questions. For once material and production saw eye to eye."

One of the major decisions made was to cut down the number of conveyor lines from six to four in the trim department and to extend the four lines, thus broadening the aisles and allowing for more convenient "off-line" storage. Lengthening these lines would cut right into the raw materials area. A member of the maintenance department stated:

"In the old days, making a change like this would have started a battle between the two production departments and also with the materials department and those of us in plant engineering. This time nobody was on the defensive. *The goal wasn't just to think with department blinders on, but it was to get the job done for the benefit of the whole show.*"

A basic change in material-handling policy was made. Materials were stored in "back-up" areas closer to the line. Delivery of materials was put on a more controlled schedule basis. A new type of stock container for individual operators was installed together with an improved system of parts identification using colored tabs and parts display boards. These changes resulted in a minimum of stock at the point of operation and "more space, better visibility, and improved layout for the operators." Greater control of materials was achieved from points of entry in the plant to individual work stations. A union committeeman noted: "That new color-code system for identifying materials made a big impression on all of us, and, *as usual, we knew all about it when it came in because Cooley had talked it all over with supervision and with the union.*"

Mention has already been made of the change in the receiving room as part of the rebuilding program. Apart from its effects on working conditions, the new setup allowed for the unloading of four to six trucks at a time for incoming shipments of parts. The installation of elevator platforms eliminated the previous costly material-handling procedure.

Although by no means unique to this plant (it was division-wide), the replacement of heavy and obsolete hand tools by lighter tools was accomplished as quickly as possible. Electric power requirements for improved lighting and other facilities throughout the plant forced the addition of a new power substation and later a new powerhouse.

A corollary effect of the physical changes was to eleminate, so supervision reported, the extreme sense of emergency. Almost all of the foremen and general foremen interviewed made comments similar to those of the general foreman who said:

> "With all those little changes and big changes, we have more time to get around. And with more time we can think a little bit more about planning, instead of worrying what's going to happen the next minute. This may sound like small stuff, and I suppose if you take any one of the changes it probably is a small thing, but if you work out in the shop, you can see these small things are important. As they kept making different changes, these small changes had a way of snowballing. Each one gives us that much more chance to think ahead so that we don't get into a hole the next time. Also, it was when the men saw some of these changes being made that they began to believe that we were trying to do something for them. You can talk a lot about human relations, but unless you can show something that you have done, why it is only a lot of talk. We used to get that talk in the old training sessions, but it didn't mean anything."

Several typical themes are brought out by this comment. One is that change was not sudden and dramatic, but was a product of many small physical changes. Another theme is that improvements in operations allowed supervision more time to plan. Notice further that the general foreman deprecates the value of "human relations" training as "only a lot of talk" if it is not linked to tangible action.

Many foremen made similar comments about the effects of physical changes on attitudes and "human relations." They were saying, in effect, that greater motivation was not a consequence of more rewarding interpersonal relationships alone; they placed equal stress on the elimination of technical "bottlenecks" as a rewarding experience in itself, a condition which in turn reduced the potential for interpersonal conflict. As one foreman put it:

> "I don't think I know how to say what brought all this about. It's hard to explain. It's like a chain reaction, and you can't put your finger on any one thing. You fix up materials, and that does one thing. And you get better tools, and that helps in another way. The thing builds up after a while. It ain't perfect yet, but we're getting some place. It seems like every single section foreman on the line is trying to run his section the best way he can for the whole line. All of us are more willing to get along because there are fewer reasons for squawking at each other.

Implicit in this comment and many others like it was that improvements in the physical work flow had an effect not only on performance but on attitudes as well. And as the attitudes changed there was increased interest in making plans for further physical changes. The quotation above repeats some of the observations made by those in higher echelons, and it also brings out a familiar theme expressed by all foremen: that they were working to make the *total* operation function more efficiently, not just their own separate sections of the line. More will be said about this later, but it is appropriate to observe in passing that this shift away from thinking of one's personal specialty alone toward a broader interest in "the whole line" is one of the more significant changes at Plant Y.

# CHAPTER 5

# Plant Y in 1956

## A. *VERTICAL RELATIONS IN THE PRODUCTION ORGANIZATION*

In the earlier section on interpersonal relations in 1953, which described the various levels of the line organization from division to plant manager and plant manager down through production foreman, certain observations were made which can be used as benchmarks for describing interpersonal relations in 1956.

It was noted that in 1953 the manager was "under pressure" from division officials. Because of the plant's failure to perform properly the plant manager was subject to frequent orders, directions, and admonitions originating at the division. While the manager often questioned the legitimacy of the division's actions (to himself, not to his superiors) he nevertheless made every effort to carry out orders. In issuing orders to subordinates, he relied on his formal powers as the head of the plant to stimulate action. Subordinates perceived the manager's behavior as being primarily punishment-centered, and, since they did not consider such behavior legitimate, they withheld the transmission of much information to him. The pattern of issuance of orders, arbitrary rule enforcement, and reliance on formal authority was observed at all levels. The sentiments expressed by all members were generally negative.

"Everybody cuts the other guy's throat in supervision."

"The plant operates in a constant atmosphere of suspicion and pressure."

"The foremen don't make decisions."

By 1956 the entire pattern of vertical relations had changed substantially with no change in the formal structure (number of levels, departmental functions, position descriptions, etc.).

Using the qualitative comments of members of the line organization, this section proceeds along somewhat the lines of the description of vertical relations in 1953. At first, general attitudinal comments about the total situation will be made, followed by a discussion of the manager's role as perceived by subordinates, the relation of subordinates to superiors below the manager, and the perception by superiors of subordinate behavior. The final section under vertical relations will include lateral or peer relations at the foreman level.

Before proceeding it is important to restate that we are dealing here with emotionally charged qualitative information. We are quoting what members of the organization said to this observer without necessarily accepting the substance of many observations they make. As one may have supposed from the preceeding chapter, the reaction of supervision to the improved situation in 1956 was entirely favorable: it may even be described as "euphoric." It sounds "almost too good to be true." As will be shown later, the dramatic improvement in performance strongly indicates that the members of the managerial group not only *felt* different about their "new life" at Plant Y; they *behaved* in a different manner. Undoubtedly some dissatisfactions and interpersonal frictions persisted, but, because the favorable aspects were so much more impressive to them, these dissatisfactions and frictions were relatively unimportant.

### 1. General Attitudinal Comments

A central theme in almost all of the 1956 interviews was that fear was no longer the primary motivating force behind the actions and responses of the members of supervision. It was a common practice for individuals to contrast the conditions of the two time periods. As one superintendent observed:

"A lot of people apparently think that this plant was not a successful plant in the old days. I don't think this is quite true. There were times when this plant was not too bad. But all I can say is that success, whatever we had of success, was paid for at a great cost. What a cost! How was it done? Out and out fear. This plant ran on fear and fear alone. Get me straight now. We still have intense competition with the other plants, and in a way that's a kind of fear, but nobody today who knows he's doing a reasonably good job has any fear of losing his job. Fear in the old days was based on the simple principle, 'If you can't do it, get out.'"

A foreman generalized his feelings about fear and pressure by saying: "The way I look at it is this. Before, it was push, push, push, all the time. Now, it's go, go, go, but that's a different thing, if you get what I mean." He went on to explain that in former days he took action on some immediate problem only when he was either ordered to do so, or when he realized that failure to act would bring on some punishment by his superior. Under the new conditions, he felt an internal compulsion to want to act and to make innovations "on his own hook." He felt free to make suggestions to his superiors.

The expressed sense of release was revealed in other ways. Supervisors often observed that ideas for improving the organization had long existed in their minds, but that these ideas could not be expressed because of the prevailing "climate of fear." One superintendent put it:

"What happened around here, as I see it, is that what they have tried to do is to formalize in a program many of the things which the best supervisors did in the first place. The trouble was in the old days that what some of the best foremen did was often frowned upon. Today we operate in the open and do many of the things that we used to have to hide."

Another broad theme which the respondents continually stressed, as they observed a general shift in attitudes, was that the change came slowly. They often made a distinction between the swift change in attitudes toward one person—the manager—following his succession to office, and the slow change in attitudes toward or perceptions about their immediate superiors, subordinates, and peers. They indicated that they had to go through many experiences—*successful* experiences in solving technical problems—before fear and distrust of the intentions of their superiors could be eliminated. A general foreman expressed it this way:

"It's hard to explain the reason for what has happened. There was no sudden overturn. Just gradually we learned how to do the job, how to take care of things one at a time. In an outfit like this you can change the speed of the conveyor by pushing a couple of buttons, but you can't do that with people. It's like a kid riding a bike. He has to do it time and time again before he gets the hang of it. I had to feel that those above me were trying to act a little more human. It's been a great improvement."

### 2. *Subordinates' Relations with the Plant Manager*

There can be little doubt that the new manager's behavior as perceived by subordinates had a marked effect on all interpersonal relations. Whereas in 1953 almost every reference to the former manager was antagonistic, not one among all comments of the 1956 interviews reflected any antagonistic feelings toward the new manager.

A general foreman, who in 1953 condemned the manager for "never listening" and for promoting "too much feeling of superiority in rank," drew the following contrast:

"When I talked with you last time, I had just about reached a point of thinking that all the things I believed in were wrong. I had always believed that if you treat people right, you will be treated the right way. I was under the impression that this was the way to operate. But then I began to believe that my whole thinking was wrong and that I should pattern myself after the way the people on top operated. I couldn't resolve this conflict within myself and started to make inquiries about a job outside. [laugh] Now I'm convinced that I was dead right because that's just the way we are operating in this organization, from the top down now."

In describing how the manager's behavior "set the pattern"

for the entire organization, several supervisors stressed the manager's belief in the "worth of the individual." A general foreman remarked, "It's just the general approach he has toward everything, and it goes right down through the organization." The foreman added: "He feels that a fellow is an individual and you have to treat him as an individual, and he means it."

The way in which members of supervision regarded the manager's informal visits and conversations with foremen on the shop floor stood in sharp contrast to their opinions of similar activities of the former manager in the earlier period. They regarded these face-to-face contacts as a means of exchanging technical ideas or of "socializing" and as not being for the purpose of punishment. The new manager avoided in his words and in his dress any display of superior status. Here are some typical random comments of foremen.

"What a difference! Like night and day. The manager comes down and jokes a lot. That's something we never had before."

"This plant has improved 100 per cent, and I think it's mostly the manager. He walks around the plant and talks with the men. He just wears an old beatup jacket and doesn't act superior."

"The manager goes all over the plant and speaks to everybody. Not the way it used to be. He comes up and says 'good morning' to me and the men, and he means it."

"The foremen all know he is pulling for the foremen and has a lot of respect for the foremen's judgment."

"The foreman knows that if he's got the stuff, he's going to be recognized and promoted. He knows top management wants to help the foreman get ahead."

This "promotion" theme was mentioned often in 1956, rarely in 1953. In 1953 emphasis was on job survival alone. No one expressed the hope of advancing in the organization; no one expressed even the desire to advance.

### 3. Superior/Subordinate Relations below the Plant Manager

Changes in vertical relations were not limited to the behavior of the manager directly toward those at lower levels. By 1956 a marked change in superior/subordinate relations below the manager level had taken place. Three general observations can be made. First, the expressed opinions of superiors toward subordinates and of subordinates toward superiors were more positive and favorable than they were in 1953. Second, a greater amount of information was flowing upward from subordinate to superior; subordinates said that they had "easier access" to superiors. Third, a greater proportion of communications concerned future planning rather than present emergencies.

The first group of comments below reflects how subordinates (mostly foremen) perceived their new relationship to superiors.

### a) Subordinates View Their Superiors

Stressing the change by general foremen and superintendents from "punitive" to "rewarding" behavior, foremen made the following typical comments:

"Upper supervision has improved a lot. Our superintendent now couldn't be better, the general foreman has mellowed quite a bit, and it's quite good now. I can't say that I talk with him more often on an average day, but the times that we do talk are constructive instead of putting me on the spot. They understand the foremen's problems and the operators' problems, and as a result of this, it helps both the foremen and the men."

"The general foreman in the old days used to come around and say to a foreman, 'Throw that bum out on the street.' Quite a change now. The general foreman will now come up when there is a problem with a man and ask you whether the man has been shown just what his job does to other operations. He checks to find out whether the man has his tools and everything he needs. Only after some exploring to make sure that I've done all I could in my power does he attempt to make a decision. He will help the foreman to decide what further action to take. This may take time, but I think it pays off. The general foreman is taking more time."

Foremen believed that general foremen and superintendents

were helpful in solving technical problems by concentrating on the problem rather than on fixing blame on the foremen. As one foreman said:

> "When there is trouble, their attitude is to find out what the problem is first. They don't take it out on the men or the foremen as the scapegoat, but they take it out on the problem first. There are some people around here who I used to think were real bastards, but they have changed quite a lot."

Foremen often observed that with additional information and help from superiors they were in a better position to make their own decisions without interference from above:

> "In the old days the general foremen and the superintendent were pretty arbitrary in telling us how many men we should have on the line. Now, the superintendent comes down and we talk about it. We still have to watch our labor costs, but a lot of it is left up to the foreman. The big thing is that us foremen are taken into confidence now. It's better teamwork."

Two of the twenty-five foremen interviewed, however, expressed concern about their relationship to their immediate superiors or to the superintendents. They feared that if it were not for the pattern set by the plant manager, some members of middle management would return to their former tactics of using threats of punishment. In other words, they perceived what they thought was a superficial behavior change but not a fundamental attitude change. One of them said:

> "Some of the older supervisors were smart enough to see the handwriting on the wall and changed when they got the new regime. I believe that a lot of them have changed, and there are a lot of them who have not changed. I'm talking about some of the general foremen and superintendents. Some of them act like they are just willing to go along, *but if there should be a change in top management, they could slide right back into their old ways.* That old horsewhip attitude is still underneath with some people, but they manage to hide it."

The other foreman, when asked if he had noticed any change in his relationship to his general foreman, said:

"Top management from the superintendent up certainly act a lot better toward us foremen than they ever did before. But it is middle management, the general foremen, who I think are the same. It's the man the foremen works for that counts, and that's the general foreman. The general foremen, a lot of them, still act the same way; the only time you see them is when they're coming down to bawl you out for something. They don't bother me, but they bother some of the younger foremen. People have respect for themselves, and they don't like to be stepped on. If they're stepped on, they feel like snapping right back."

### b) Superiors View Their Subordinates

The observations above were made by subordinates. How superiors in the production group regarded their subordinates was also important.

Many recognized the tendency in the former period for those at higher levels to "hold the reins" on decisions and not trust those at lower levels. As one general foreman put it:

"I don't know how to explain how it was back then. It was like being sick, and it took time to grow out of it. Management has been good. They hold the reins, but still they let us run our own show, and I let my foremen run *their* own show."

A superintendent cited an example to illustrate his trust in the ability of his subordinates to run departmental operations without him:

"I could leave right now and not worry about how the job would be done. I have men under me now who could do all right without me. For instance, toward the end of the baseball season seven of us, including two superintendents, left the plant to go to a ball game. That's something I have never been able to do in this plant before. The fellows who took over did a good job that day, maybe in order to shame me, which we liked."

General foremen also often cited examples to illustrate how they had come to trust their foremen to manage their sections with a minimum of interference from above. One of them, after recalling that formerly "I insisted that the foremen make no moves without consulting me," said:

"Now I don't worry all the time about my foremen getting me into hot water. They have the kind of information which allows them to see beyond the next minute or the next hour. My job is to help them get what they need. I'm not as rushed, so I can spend more time listening to what they have to say. The more I do this, the more I realize what good men they really are when they have half a chance to do a job."

The theme of trust in subordinates was expressed by the foremen themselves as they discussed their relationship to the hourly operators. As two of them observed:

"Years back when someone did something wrong, the attitude was 'throw him out.' Now there is a different attitude. We take the *time* that it takes to break a man in. How long has he been on a job? How well is he broken in? We take time to do more teaching on the job now. Management shows respect for the men, and the men respect management for it, too."

"I've noticed a real difference in the hourly workers. They seem a lot more willing to work, and I can't explain just why it is, but something happened all right. I suppose it's being treated better. My boss treats me better because he gets treated better. People above me listen to me, and I hope, at least, that I listen to my people below me."

### 4. *Peer Relations at the Foreman Level*

A change in reciprocal attitudes of superiors and subordinates in the production organization was paralleled by a marked change in peer relations. Superintendents were not only meeting together weekly in the scheduled cost and quality meetings, but they often met informally to notify one another about potential interdepartmental problems. General foremen also cited instances of sharing information which was useful to a group of sections, not just their own. "We broke through the wall of secrecy and suspicion" is the way one of them put it.

The largest proportion of comments about peer relationships came from the foremen. As was pointed out earlier, the continuous workflow principle requires that a certain amount of horizontal information flow from one foreman's section to the next. Considerable intersectional hostility had been observed in the 1953 period; this often resulted in a foreman's withholding information from the foremen in preceding or succeeding operations. The contrast between the periods is revealed by typical quotes of two of the production foremen:

> "One of the best things that I feel has happened around here is the co-operation between foremen in different sections. It used to be that when a poor operation came through from another section, the foreman's attitude [in a subsequent section] was, and I know it was true with me too, 'That's his worry.' Now we try to grab it and tell the foreman about it. Just yesterday I had some stuff going through to the next foreman which wasn't too good, but I was on the spot because the operator on a particular job wasn't too good. The foreman in the next section came up to me and told me not to worry about it, and that he would have his men fix the thing up for the time being."

> "When we had all that pressure on us a few years back we used to bark at each other all the time, but not now. When the pressure is off, you can think and do a better job, and you get along better with the other foremen. We still have plenty of pressure, but it's not the kind that makes you do things you don't want to do. Or put it another way: when the pressure is on, there is a good reason for it, not just some boss trying to pull rank on you."

## B. RELATIONS OF PRODUCTION TO NONPRODUCTION GROUPS

A complex production organization, such as an automobile assembly plant, requires large numbers of persons who do not "produce" the product itself. As outlined previously, there are roughly three different types of nonproduction functions: those involving service, control, and reporting.

In the three years from 1953 to 1956, a change in the relationship between the production and nonproduction groups took place, even though their respective roles as set forth in formal manuals and charts were identical in both periods. The change did not come about overnight, but started slowly, first at one level or area, then another. The nonproduction departments whose activities are of direct concern to the production departments include material control, work standards, inspection, maintenance (or plant engineering), and accounting.

## 1. *Material Control*

As was indicated earlier controlling the schedule and flow of several hundred thousand parts and materials through the assembly line is an extremely difficult problem in logistics. Failure of parts to arrive at the right section of the two-mile-long conveyor at the right time could have serious consequences, even to the extent of shutting down operations entirely. It is the primary duty of material control to establish schedules and to see to it that materials are fed on schedule from the loading platforms and storage areas to the line. At this point, those in operating departments take over.

During the first few months of the new administration the plant manager and production manager, in their frequent visits to the production floor, heard numerous complaints about the chronic material shortages, the poor arrangement of facilities for storing materials on the line, the irregular schedule, and many other problems. They recognized that both the production supervisors and those in the material control group were spending too much of their time complaining to one another about immediate crises.

Individual members of both groups offered many suggestions as to how the system of material control and production schedules could be changed. However, there was little evidence that these ideas had ever been drawn together systematically, discussed, and then implemented.

In one of the staff meetings late in 1953, the decision was made to assign some members of the material control and the production departments "to study the material bottlenecks, especially in the trim department." These men proceeded jointly to question foremen, general foremen, and material handlers and to observe in detail the precise sequence of material and parts movement from loading platform to the line.

The significance of these discussions is suggested by a comment from one of the trim department general foremen: "This was the first time I had a chance to talk with material department people without getting into a cat and dog fight."

The head of material control drew up a series of recommendations which were discussed at a staff meeting. One of the recommendations concerned the arrangement of materials along the various stations of the line. The action which followed is described by the manager:

> "The immediate objective was to get order in the place. So we laid out on paper where the racks should be placed and who was responsible for maintaining order in each area. The end goal was a practical layout for each type of material with a method of follow-up checks to measure progress."

Within the first year this and several other recommendations were carried out. It was observed that at each step not only were production and material personnel informed about the plans, but the advice of others in nonoperating departments was sought.

In order to give members of the material control department some perspective on the progress of the plans as they were put into effect, the weekly material department meetings referred to earlier were begun during this period. The comptroller for the plant presented figures to all supervisors and clerks showing "the progress from one week to the next . . . and figures which measured the material-handling costs at a given week against the year to date."

To remedy a chronic complaint by the foremen ("We never know what our own material costs are") the cost information was broken down by each foreman's section. As one member of management put it: "In time we had it worked out so that there was a given clerk in the material department to whom the foreman could go and check his specific costs."

By 1956 most of the expressed antagonism between operating supervision and the material control group had disappeared. In each interview, comments such as those of the following superintendent and a foreman were recorded thus:

"The big headaches we used to have over material shortages have been eliminated. We still have some, but it doesn't last very long. The big reason is the 'control.' The material department people and those of us in production spend a lot of time just working up what the best control should be. The material department, I am sure, has a lot better co-operation from the production department."

"Getting the right material when we need it and where we need it is no longer one of our big problems. In switching people around, they have some new men in there who really try to break their backs to help. Nowadays, whenever I run short of materials, I just call them and they tell me they'll have the stuff for me in fifteen minutes."

In the earlier period, large proportions of a production foreman's time had been spent "tracking down" holdups in the flow of materials to his section. He had been constantly ordering the stock chaser assigned to his section to bring in parts and materials. He had frequently complained to his general foremen about the chronic condition of "shortages." At the same time, he had been ordered by his superiors to keep up his production and reduce costs. When he had communicated with others he had been concerned almost exclusively with "getting off the hook" on some emergency.

By 1956 communications of this type had sharply declined, not simply because operating supervision and those in material control had somehow learned to "get along with each other"; rather, the sources of difficulty in a purely technical sense had been largely eliminated. Parts and materials were being delivered on time in good condition and were conveniently placed and clearly indentified at the various assembly stations.

The foremen's activities with respect to material control matters shifted from having to handle emergencies to planning that would obviate emergencies. In carrying out these activities, the foremen, and indeed all members of operating supervision, talked frequently with clerks and supervisors in material control about future actions to improve the system.

This condition resulted in a change in the way major decisions were made in the top echelons. Recommendations for action were introduced to the manager and his staff, having already been thoroughly discussed among those at lower levels. In the earlier period, information on a particular problem often came to the manager's attention from two separate sources—from operating departments and from the material control department. Each would present its own "case" in explaining the source of the difficulty. The manager would then make a decision based on the separate arguments. Under the new administration a number of alternative proposals might be submitted to the manager, usually having been drawn up jointly.

## 2. Inspection

The relationship of inspection to production at PlantY was, on paper at least, identical under both old and new administrations. The job of inspection essentially was to say "this will pass" or "this will not pass." As suggested earlier, this kind of condition by its very nature can lead to considerable friction. It is a familiar "institutional point of conflict."

The study of 1953 had revealed widespread expressions of antagonism between the two groups. The plant manager and chief inspector had been under constant pressure from the division to "clamp down" on the quality of the product. The chief inspector had issued orders down through his department to inspection foremen and to hourly inspectors. The production manager "put the squeeze" on the line organization down through foremen to hourly operators. It was noted further that members of the inspection organization in different geographical areas rarely communicated with each other as a group. As a result, decisions as to what could or could not pass varied considerably. Inspectors on the line would say "yes" to a particular job, while final inspectors were saying "no" to the same job.

The process of change in the relationship of these two groups closely parallels the change occurring in other production/nonproduction relationships. The first phase began with direct and informal conversations on the shop floor between the manager and members of both groups. Then weekly meetings instituted by the manager were attended by the chief inspector and operating supervisors down through the general foreman level. At first these meetings were exploratory. Each participant was encouraged to spell out what he considered to be the critical problem areas involving quality. Later the group blocked out an outline of a training and informational program for operating and inspection foremen and for hourly inspectors. Details of procedure were then worked out among the training director, chief inspector, and other representatives of the operating departments. Ideas from the material control and work standards departments were also solicited.

The reaction to steps that were taken to improve the production/inspection relationship is reflected at the foreman level by the following typical remark in 1956:

"One of the big changes that has come about is in the way foremen and inspection people view each other. When the new management came in, they got people down here who were really trained inspectors. They came in and showed us foremen exactly how the job should be done. Before, it was hit or miss as to how to interpret the specifications. Now they can show the foremen just what is expected. We are in contact with each other a lot more, not because the quality is poorer; it isn't. But I mean we tip each other off to keep an eye out for things. This has made for a lot better feeling between the foremen and inspection. Inspection will always tell you when something is wrong, but they seem to understand the foreman's problems a little better, especially when he is loaded with a lot of absentees or when he is having a run of trouble. The inspection foreman doesn't come over and bark at me. In the old days, the inspectors on my line were never considered a part of my group. They still are not, in one sense. That is, they report up through the inspection organization. But now they act like they were part of my section. They don't look down on us. In the last year we've really had to tighten up on the quality of work because of the automobile competition, but it makes it a lot easier when you understand thoroughly just what inspection people expect of us."

Several foremen put considerable emphasis on three points made by the above foreman. The first was that operating supervision and members of the inspection department agreed with each other as to what was acceptable quality and what was not. A second related point was that communications between operating supervision and inspection were not dominated by the inspection group. "We tip each other off." That is, under former conditions, a foreman, as one of them admitted, "might just let some stuff slip by hoping it would be missed by the inspectors and fixed up later in car conditioning." In the new inspection/production relationship, the production foreman would inform inspection to keep an eye on certain kinds of jobs which were causing trouble. A third observation made by most of the foremen was the acceptance of the inspector "as part of my group." Inspectors had always been in the same area with operating personnel, but previously, as one foreman put it, "We treated them like foreigners"; they were looked upon as a threat. It was the inspector's reports to his superiors that eventually resulted in criticism and threats from the foreman's superiors. Foremen believed, and cited several examples to illustrate, that higher management consciously discouraged any "fraternization" between inspection and production. In the new relationship, foremen were encouraged to share problems with inspection. The inspector's primary function of passing on quality had not changed, but the roles which each perceived for the other *had* changed.

It is interesting to note that greater acceptance of inspectors took place in spite of the fact that quality standards had measurably stiffened during 1955 and 1956.

### 3. *Work Standards*

As in any modern factory operation, Plant Y had one department whose prescribed duties were to analyze carefully each operation on the production line, taking into consideration tools and facilities available, the nature of the material being processed, and the optimum time to be allowed for each of the series of work elements included in any given operation performed by a worker. From these data is was possible to determine how much a given operator could be expected to perform under given conditions of the line speed. Elaborate manuals and rules circumscribing the activity of the work standards department had been worked out by the company at the division level. Each plant could set its own standards within the limits of the prescribed rules.

At plant Y there was, as one member put it in 1953, "a tendency for the staff of the work standards department to dictate in some detail precisely how each foreman should arrange the job elements and operations in his own section."

Although supervisors in the 1953 period wholly accepted the use of work standards and recognized the necessity of having such standards determined by those technically qualified in time and motion study, they nevertheless thought that the "experts" did not always take all the factors into consideration in saying that a given job was too "tight" or too "loose." On the question of balancing the work load of each of the operators in the various sections of the line, the foremen in the earlier interviews had frequently expressed the belief that they, not the standards department, were the ones who should make the decision. As one of them had put it:

"I have twenty-six men in my section. As long as I don't use more than this number and as long as I don't overload any one man I should be able to distribute the work as I see it without having one of them smart time study fellows tell me what I'm supposed to do."

The new administration recognized that the rigid controls exercised by the work standards department were resented by the foremen; here was one further source of administrative control which limited the foremen's authority. After several months of discussions between the work standards department and operating supervision at all levels, a change in policy was made. As the plant manager described it:

"The foreman was made chiefly responsible for determining the work assignment of the individual worker. Before it was done in reverse. The time study man [work standards] determined the job content. The foremen would say to a man 'You have to do the job because that is what somebody tells me.' So we had to get the foreman, with agreement of the general foreman or superintendent, to assume the responsibility. The foreman had to be sold on it himself or he would never get it accepted by others. We stayed with it. The time study man was there to measure results and to advise and counsel the foreman."

A change in the union's policy also appears to have taken place with respect to disputes on work standards. As one of the principal union officers said:

"It used to be that when a complaint came up, the union would ask for a detailed breakdown of the elements and time from the standards department. Then the union would check these against their own observations. Sometimes it took more than three months to settle it. We often said that we would have to strike the plant to get agreement. Now what we do when we hear a complaint is to take a quick look at it. If a man doesn't have a gripe, we tell him. If he does, we talk to the foreman and get it settled. So, management doesn't send the time standards men out all the time."

Without exception every foreman who discussed the question of standards made positive and favorable comments. Here are three examples:

"You don't hear the same kind of yell any more about overwork. We get our share of it, but it's not nearly the same as it used to be in the old days. It used to be the practice to get in work standards and pull the clock on a man every time he yelled he had too much work. Now they keep the clocks out. They let the foremen decide whether a man has too much to do or not. In some cases, and these are special, they'll bring a clock in, but usually it is when we all agree to it, including the committeeman. In fact, I go to the [union] committeeman quite a lot now to tell him when I am going to change a job if I think a man should have another operation."

"If the foreman wants the facts, o.k.; the time standards man will come out. However, usually if there is a discrepancy, the foreman decides how to settle that discrepancy. It's not like the old days when time standards was boss. Whenever there was a grievance about overwork, the time standards man would come in and say 'This is it,' and you had to take it. The union takes more interest in the jobs now, too. Since they can discuss it with the foreman, they make suggestions about how to redistribute the elements. [An element is one unit of work comprising the totality of a worker's operations.] The committeeman might say: 'Well, this fellow is overworked; perhaps you can give it to that fellow over there. He might be able to handle this particular element.' As a foreman, I don't have to go along with the committeeman, but if you build up mutual trust, it makes it easier."

"Once in a blue moon they'll bring a standards man in, but for the most part now they leave it right up to the foreman. They trust me. Everything used to be real tight before, and the standards people pretty much dictated what was involved in an operation. The foremen were afraid to buck it. Now it's up to the foreman. If a foreman can get the stuff out in good quality and keep up the efficiency, they don't care very much how a foreman does it."

Several interpretative observations may be made about these comments by members of the production organization. The work standards department was established and maintained to perform one of the necessary control functions in the formal organization. As the comments suggest, prior to 1953, a sharp separation was made between the actions of those in the work standards department and those in the production department. Foremen were held responsible for the output of their sections, yet the determination of required manpower was relegated to another group. After 1953, with increased discussions between members of both groups under conditions in which fear of punishment was removed, it became obvious that greater control of work assignments should be given to those most directly responsible for performance—i.e., the foremen. When questions arose about "work loads," the decisions were usually left in the foremen's hands. The new role of the work standards representative was that of providing advice and information.

To summarize relationships between the production and

work standards departments in the two time periods, certain significant points can be made. Quite obviously a substantial change took place in attitudes; this change was a result of an even more basic change in the functional relationship between the two groups. In the early period, upper management, anxious to maintain rigid controls over the disposition and use of manpower, insisted that questions of manpower be handled by the time and motion experts. In carrying out this control mandate, this nonproduction department acted with direct line authority over production foremen, yet the foremen were held responsible by their own direct superiors for the performance of the workers. Repeated experience had taught them that it would do no good to "appeal their case" either to work standards representatives or to their own superiors. Upward communications were blocked. Obedience to orders, regardless of the legitimacy of the orders in the foreman's eyes, became an end in itself.

By 1956, the relationship of the work standards department and production foremen was one of collaborative effort. The work standards department was regarded by foremen as a service, rather than as a control group. Foremen communicated frequently with their counterparts in work standards, and the advice of the latter was often accepted. The new "system" of interpersonal relations made the advice "legitimate."

### 4. *Maintenance (Plant Engineering)*

To members of production departments, the role played by the maintenance department is crucially important as a service function. Not only do repairs have to be made immediately lest the line be held up, but "preventive maintenance" is also essential. From observations made in the 1953 period, activities of the plant engineering department appeared to have been poorly co-ordinated with those of the operating and other service departments. As in many other production/nonproduction relations, those in maintenance and production had tended to reflect the formal organization chart with its emphasis on separate functions and vertical communications.

These conditions and the changes which took place are illustrated by the comments of the plant engineer who held the same job in both time periods:

"The way things operated in the old days, if the production department wanted to rearrange things, they would tell plant engineering to go ahead and do it. After it was all over they would find that it made it impossible for the material department. The material department would put up a squawk, and then somebody would get hell. That all changed when we operated the new way. In the regular staff meetings it was decided that a certain area was critical to hit. We got everybody together who would be concerned. The standards department was important because a rearrangement would affect how the jobs were to be broken down. Materials had to know what the layout was going to be. With the operating people, all the details got worked out in a conference between the people at lower levels directly connected with the problem. When they reached an agreement, it would be reported up the line until it got to the top staff. We had disagreements on small things, *but for the first time everybody was interested in doing the right thing for the whole plant.*

"It did a lot to eliminate suspicion. Mat [the new plant manager] worked on the principle of letting the managers run their own departments, but he insisted that the department heads keep no secrets from the others. The former plant manager seemed to be suspicious of department heads, so everybody played their cost figures close to their chest. Now they are available to everybody."

A production department head's reaction to this was:

"I think the foremen, and it's true with me, too, feel now that we are getting a lot more help from the maintenance department. We all saw a lot of things that were wrong and would ask for help but usually didn't get it, or didn't get it when we needed it. After a while we just got discouraged and stopped trying."

The comment of the plant engineer points up many of the basic changes that were noted in other interdepartmental relationships. Previously, the activities carried out by the maintenance department had not been integrated with those of other departments. Actions by this department had been taken in response to specific demands of some particular department (or of the manager) regardless of the ultimate effect on the actions of other service, control, or production groups. In one sense, the nature of the work flow demanded the constant exchange of information laterally between the different departments, but in practice these lateral exchanges had been blocked because of the manager's repeated emphasis on having information flow vertically through the separate and formal channels.

As the head of plant maintenance indicated, his relationship to other groups had changed substantially under the new manager; he no longer was forced to view his services as a distinct and separate function. His actions were taken from a more global perspective. His primary concern was the solution of technical problems in co-operation with others, not on "saving his own skin" through action calculated to please his superiors. Information on which final decisions were based was exchanged at levels closest to the particular technical problem, then submitted to higher authorities as joint recommendations. The actions which followed utilized the specialized craft skills of the maintenance group, but the exercise of such skills was integrated with the needs of the total organization. Doing the "right thing for the plant" replaced what was formerly "doing the right thing for the department—the maintenance department."

### 5. *The Comptroller's Department*

One of the major control activities in any industrial organization is that of accounting. Budgets and cost figures dictate to a great extent what the organization as a whole or the individual supervisors in it can or cannot do. The most direct link between the local assembly plant and the corporation is through the comptroller. At Plant Y, members of local management were fully aware that even though the plant comptroller, for administrative purposes, reported to the plant manager, he had to enforce rules and regulations set at higher corporate levels.

A frequent complaint heard from operating supervision in 1953 and previously was that the information coming down from the comptroller's office, with particular respect to efficiency reports, had been misunderstood, meaningless, and as one member of mangement put it, "downright harmful." Members of operating supervision recognized that in order to operate efficiently, it was critically necessary to have periodic information which would allow them to know whether or not they were operating according to their budget and according to standards. However, they felt that the figures showing poor efficiency had been used by top plant management as a personal indictment of their particular operation, when, in fact, the inefficiencies had often been caused by circumstances beyond their control. The comptroller's department had been looked upon as a distant impersonal group of accounting machines whose personnel understood little and cared less about the practical usefulness of figures to the operating departments. Because these figures had been used as a "bludgeon" by the plant manager, supervisors had come to look upon the comptroller with deep fear and suspicion. As the plant engineer observed: "Everyone played the cost figures close to their chests."

By 1956 the relationship between operating supervision and members of the comptroller's department had changed considerably. "Being in the know" was a frequent remark heard from supervision with respect to cost control figures. The process by which this change came about has many parallels in the changes observed in other functional relationships.

How the change process came about is best illustrated by the following detailed comments of the comptroller himself:

> "You know, most people in the shop always think of the comptroller as someone up in some corner office dealing with a lot of mysterious figures, and getting out financial statements, and making payrolls, and that's about all. This is perhaps common to the operation of any comptroller, but I recognized soon after I got to Plant Y that I would have a chance to do some of the things I long wanted to do. Mat Cooley told me right off that he felt

that our department could be a lot more helpful to the operating people and the service departments. In fact, the way it worked out he [the manager] would frequently come up and grab me and tell me that we were going to take a walk through the plant. There were several weeks in which we went through the plant together two and three times a week, sometimes twice a day.

"I spent a lot of time talking not only to the department heads and the superintendents, but with the general foremen and all other foremen as well. I spent a lot of my time trying to find out what the figures that came out of my department meant to the operating and service departments, and then discussing ways in which those figures could be more meaningful. I tried to demonstrate what was behind the figures and how we calculated them, but it became apparent that, although they got to understand how the information on efficiency and costs and other things was constructed, they were not necessarily the types of information which would be useful to them in their day-to-day work. We found so often, when you really got the foremen to open up, they thought that some of our figures were lying. The figures in themselves were not wrong, but they certainly weren't useful to them, which amounts to about the same thing. For example, if you simply come out with a figure and tell a foreman that he is 10 per cent over standard costs, that doesn't mean too much to him unless he understands why. As we found out in our talks with the foremen, there could be six or seven different factors which would account for a foreman's being over standard, and some of these factors could be beyond his control. Yet he was punished for them when they were beyond his control. We worked a long time figuring up a formula which the foremen and general foremen and superintendents could use to analyze efficiency figures quickly. Also, we broke down the efficiencies, after we got the over-all figures, into individual elements and laid a program out on that basis. Next, we got all of supervision in and presented the idea to them, showing that the idea had basically come from our talks with them.

"Our experience proved to me that a carefully devised system of financial control is not necessarily a real system of cost control. Real cost control operates on the philosophy that we adopted for the supervisors responsible for the different areas. In other words, the first thing to do is to get to know their needs as they see them and give them the figures that are tailored to these needs. At the same time, of course, we continue to send to central headquarters, all the weekly and monthly reports in just the form which the division and the corporation requires."

From the comptroller's remarks, certain phases in the change process may be discerned. The first phase was marked by direct and informal contacts of the comptroller and plant manager with foremen, general foremen, and other supervisors. From these contacts the comptroller learned that the accounting control systems were not only misunderstood but that they were regarded as a further threat to a supervisor's job security.

In the second phase, the comptroller and his staff sought to explain how the system worked and how the figures used to measure efficiency were obtained. It became apparent that regardless of how much the system was explained, members of supervision questioned the usefulness of the figures for their own particular operations. They continued to view the accounting function as something required by the division and corporation for purposes which were of no direct help to plant-level supervision.

The third phase saw the comptroller and his department establish a system of reporting which was based on the immediate needs of plant supervision. He was, of course, required by regulations to maintain a rigid and standardized reporting system according to procedures laid down by higher authorities, but paralleling this system he instituted another method of internal reporting.

Notice that the new system evolved from many discussions with those who would be most directly affected. It was looked upon as a measure of assistance, and not simply as another set of "red tape" regulations.

Members of supervision reported that the new system introduced a degree of predictability which had not been possible before. As in the case of other changes which took place at Plant Y, the increase in the time perspective made it possible to plan and such planning reduced the number of daily crises.

The increased co-ordination between the comptroller's

group and other members of the organization had an important effect on Plant Y's relationship to the division. All of the major physical changes which improved Plant Y's performance required approval of the division. The comptroller's department was ultimately responsible for "presenting the case" for division approval. The comptroller described how increased involvement in technical decisions helped him in requesting appropriations for capital outlays. As he described it:

"I got into another kind of activity which is different from the kind usually thought of for a comptroller. Cooley would often bring me in when they were going to make some kind of rearrangement in the shop. Take like in the trim department when we made those big changes. I and my people would often go down as a group with Cooley and the heads of other operating and service departments. We would observe the operations themselves to see why the changes needed to be made. Even though I didn't know much about the operations themselves, I was always asked to express my opinion. My job, of course, was to work up the information to be submitted to the division for money outlays. It meant a lot more to us, in writing up the request for appropriations, when we had the actual experience of seeing the problem itself and in having a part in making suggestions. In other words, we again got away from the business of sitting in an office by ourselves. We were cut in on the deal."

By being "cut in on the deal" members of the comptroller's department were in a position to present a more convincing case to the division and, as it happened, almost no requests were denied.

In viewing the over-all change in the relationship between this control department and the rest of the plant, it should be noted that in both time periods the formal structure and function of the department, as set down in charts, position descriptions, and in divisional manuals, underwent virtually no change. It was in the area of uncharted activities in which the most substantial changes were noted. These new activities came about as a response to the internal needs of the plant and to the external requirements of the larger organization.

# CHAPTER 6

# Before and After: Patterns of Interaction, Sentiments, and Performance

Using everyday language to describe what took place in this industrial plant, we have placed considerable reliance on events and relations as perceived and described by the participants themselves. It remains to stand a bit farther back from the running story and to gain some perspective on the essential differences between the Plant Y of 1953 and the "same" organization of 1956. Obviously the relationships among those managing the system changed substantially, but can we see any pattern to the change? Can we introduce any quantitative evidence, even if only crudely derived, showing how interactions between individuals and groups differed from one period to the next? What meaningful contrasts can be made in the expressed attitudes and feelings which the members held toward one another? And most important, what is the *proof* that the organization did in fact change when measured by performance results?

To answer these questions the material will be organized around three categories of description: "interaction," "sentiment," and "performance."[1] Other word symbols might have been used, but these appeared to be general enough to include all dimensions of behavior and specific enough to highlight the differences between two "system states," Plant Y in 1953 and Plant Y in 1956. Our concern here is with the "before" and "after," not with the process of moving from one state to another. This follows later.

---

[1] These terms are borrowed from George C. Homans, *The Human Group*, p. 34, except that Homans calls performance the "results of activity."

## A. *INTERACTION*

The survival of any living organism depends upon the ongoing interactions of its component parts. In a human group the elementary parts are people. The relationship between the members of the group may be described in many ways and at different levels of abstraction, the simplest and least abstract involving direction, frequency, and duration of interpersonal contacts. As used here the term "interaction" describes an occurence involving two or more people in which the actions of one person stimulate a reaction by another (or others). By definition interaction involves *direction* from one person, the originator, to another, the responder. A distinction is made between initiation of interaction with no response and initiation which causes the responder to take some kind of action. All contacts between one person and another cannot be considered as completed interactions; there must be some kind of action following a contact. If the response of A to a contact by B (or to a situation) is to do nothing, then the interaction is not complete; something has blocked the response. Interactions usually take place in paired events (one person originating for another). They also take place in set events (one person originating for two or more persons). *Frequency*, the number of times events take place between two or more people, is also implied. And in any given event there is a time element—the *duration* of the interpersonal contact.

Direction, frequency, and duration of interaction are capable of being observed and given mathematical symbols of measurement. Arensberg,[2] Chapple and Coon,[3] Homans,[4] Whyte,[5] Richardson[6] and others have done just this. In the present study direct and constant observation was not pos-

---

[2] Conrad M. Arensberg, "Behavior and Organization: Industrial Studies," in John H. Rohrer and Muzafer Sherif (eds.), *Social Psychology at the Crossroads.*

[3] Eliot D. Chapple and Carleton Coon, *Principles of Anthropology.*

[4] Homans, *op. cit.*

[5] William F. Whyte, "Framework for the Analysis of Industrial Relations," *Industrial and Labor Relations Review*, Vol. 3, No. 3 (April, 1950).

[6] Frederick L. W. Richardson and Charles R. Walker, *Human Relations in an Expanding Company;* and F. L. W. Richardson, *Talk, Work, and Action.*

sible,[7] and interactional data have been derived from statements by those interviewed. The most that can be expected are generalized statements about what appeared to be typical differences in the interaction patterns of the two time periods. Further, the presentation is not wholly free of comments about the content of interactions and the circumstances under which they occurred. The inclusion of content might not be acceptable to a "pure" interactionist. Yet the use of interaction as an analytical device, however crudely applied, was found to be one among several useful ways of describing this social system in two time periods.

## 1. *The General Pattern*

As one views interpersonal events in 1953 from the division level to the plant manager and down through the hierarchy to the lowest levels of supervision, it is apparent that members of the organization acted primarily in response to actions initiated by their superiors; the *direction* was predominantly downward. In 1953 there were approximately five superior-originated interactions for every one subordinate-originated interaction (based on possible analysis of 36 of the 48 respondents). In 1956 the ratio was approximately two to one (based on possible analysis of 31 out of 43 respondents). It is difficult to say precisely whether the total number of interactions—that is, *frequency*, regardless of direction—increased or decreased by 1956. Certain types of interactions decreased, while others increased. Here one must consider the conditions and content. A reduction in technical difficulties substantially reduced the need to interact in emergencies. The number of

---

[7] The magnitude of the task of direct observation of interactions may be illustrated by one study conducted under the author's direction. Each of fifty-six production foremen in an assembly plant was observed for an eight-hour day. Every incident which lasted fifteen seconds or more was recorded and coded. In all, 32,652 behavioral incidents were recorded. Approximately 20,000 of these events involved interpersonal interactions which were coded according to origination (direction), duration, and frequency, plus four other categories (topic, activity, place, and person). To have done the same thing in the present study involving several levels and departments would have made it virtually impossible to have acquired the detailed interview material upon which this study is based. See R. H. Guest, "Of Time and the Foreman," *Personnel*, Vol. 32, No. 6 (May, 1956), p. 478.

orders and directives from the division, the plant manager, and each level of supervision decreased. On the other hand, there was an increase in the number of interactional events involving planning and the transmission of technical and administrative information vertically (up and down) and horizontally (among sections and departments). This was reported by all but two of the 43 respondents in 1956. On balance, and considering the state of "chronic emergency" existing in 1953, there is reason to believe that the gross volume of interaction was *less* in 1956.

As to the average duration of face-to-face interactions, there appears to have been a much greater number of longer two-way discussions in 1956. A reduction in work-flow problems increased the availability of time for such exchanges of information.

A final general comment: The *number* of individuals with whom a given person interacted appears to have increased by 1956.[8] Several members said they had gotten to know more people in the "front office" and in other staff departments. Interdepartmental meetings brought them together. Long-range planning, a key factor in Plant Y's success, required the exchange of information among many persons and groups. A high rate of transfers meant that the individuals involved came to know more people.

## 2. *Vertical Interactions*

### *a) The Two Managers Compared*

As agent of the division and corporation and as head of the subordinate organization each manager held a key position in the system of communications. From what each reported and from comments by those at higher and lower levels, the pattern of interaction linking them to superiors and to subordinates showed marked differences. Plant Y in 1953, and especially the manager, was subject to constant inquiries or directives from above. Stewart, the manager in the early

---

[8] Reported in 1956 by nineteen of the twenty-five who were foremen in 1953.

period, rarely initiated requests for action from the division, whereas Cooley often sought and received support from headquarters. That the frequency of all contacts between division and plant appears to have been reduced is suggested by observations of division staff members such as, "Plant Y (1953) is our biggest headache and we have to keep in touch all the time." Later in 1956, he said, "Our contacts with Plant Y are routine. The critical spot now is Plant D." What does seem clear is that, whatever the frequency rate, the proportion of interactions originated *from* division *to* plant manager was higher in 1953 than in 1956. The way it was often expressed by the manager and his staff in 1956 was, "They're letting us run our own show."

The patterns of interaction between the two managers and those in the upper levels of supervision were different from each other. Five production department heads and seven non-production heads in 1953, and the incumbents of the same positions in 1956, reported approximately the same number of contacts with the manager in an average week (ranging between three and fourteen). However, only one of the twelve in 1953 indicated that contacts to and from the manager were "fifty-fifty." In 1956 most of the higher supervisors indicated a balance in the direction (initiation) of interactions with the manager.

The new manager and his subordinates interacted in set events (groups) much more frequently than had the former manager. It is true that the former manager had often summoned two or more members for emergency meetings, but no individual had met with the manager as often and as regularly over an extended period of time as was the case with the new manager's regularly scheduled meetings. To the members of the organization the function of the meetings not only increased the frequency of interaction within the group and between the staff members and the manager, but also the fact of *regularity* was seen as having a stabilizing effect on the group and on the entire organization. Agendas could be planned. Recommendations leading to decisions could be considered in advance. A sense of order without constraint developed.

These meetings provided a new interaction mechanism which had not been present earlier and which reinforced the pattern existing between the manager and others in day-to-day administrative activities. That is, they were a means by which subordinates could "originate" to the manager, as well as the reverse. Reports from those attending the meetings contrasted them with the former *ad hoc* meetings which had been used in 1953 by the manager primarily to issue orders for action.

To compare the two managers and their relationship to subordinates simply in interaction terms is, of course, a sterile comparison unless the pattern is linked to the action preceding and following a particular interaction event. Under Stewart, lack of co-ordination in the technical organization brought about certain actions leading to "crisis" interactions. Cooley started at the other end. He first "reorganized" the interaction pattern, which led to better control of technical problems. To be sure, he made significant concrete changes on the technical side, but these were not made until changes in the interaction pattern had begun to evolve. In effect, he instituted a new way of developing, processing, and implementing technical ideas.[9]

## b) *Below the Plant Manager*

The interaction patterns of manager to the division and manager to subordinates were not unlike the patterns found at lower levels. In 1953 when foremen talked about the general foremen (and general foremen about superintendents) most of the incidents centered on actions originating from the superior. Such a pattern is understandable in the light of the emphasis placed on discipline and order giving. In 1956, with the marked reduction in production holdups, there was less need for superiors to "prod" their subordinates constantly. Twenty-one out of twenty-five foremen in 1956 indicated that general foremen were giving fewer orders to

---

[9] The author is grateful to William F. Whyte for pointing out this distinction.

the foremen and that the foremen were freer to seek action from the general foremen.

This observation is supported by what we already know about the way decisions were made under the new administration. That is, with a greater exchange of technical and administrative information at lower levels, a given problem could be solved at these levels without interference from those in higher positions. On major problems affecting many sections and large numbers of people, problems that ultimately required a decision and an order from someone at higher levels, there was less need for those at higher levels to apply "close supervision" in implementing the decision. The over-all plan of action was well understood by those at lower levels before the final decision was reached. Section meetings of foremen and general foremen, or of general foremen and superintendents, preceded the final discussions of department heads and the plant manager. When a top-level decision was made, it often took but a single general order to put the agreed-upon decision into effect. Each incumbent knew what he was to do and when it was to be done.

The reduction in technical breakdowns in time not only reduced the frequency of orders from a general foreman to a foreman, but it allowed the foremen and general foremen to discuss problems which, left unsolved, might become critical in the future. This in turn tended to prevent further technical difficulties and to require less interference (interactions originating from superiors) from above.

Much of what has been said about superior/subordinate interaction applies also to peer interactions within the production department, especially at the foreman level. The number of complaints among foremen was considerably reduced, but the incidence of information sharing was greatly increased. Foremen had more time to discuss problems and the discussions followed a more "give-and-take" pattern; the responder was more compliant to a request. There were fewer interruptions.

General foremen and superintendents also reported fewer

"complaint" contacts and more information-sharing contacts with their counterparts in other areas and departments. Formerly, upper management had stressed interdepartmental competition; peers had been looked upon as competitors. Competitors could, as one member commented, "scream at each other like a bunch of washerwomen," but it was the norm to "play your cards close to the chest" about sharing information. By 1956, it was generally recognized that highly integrated continuous-flow operations required the lateral exchange of information.

### 3. Interaction Patterns of Production to Nonproduction Groups

With respect to interactions between production and nonproduction groups, among those groups whose primary function was direct *service* to production, such as the material or maintenance groups, there was a reduction by 1956 in the total volume of interactions.[10] Improved material flow, better layout of equipment, and a sustained program of "preventive maintenance" had sharply reduced the number of breakdowns and delays. There was less need for production foremen and general foremen to make frequent emergency calls (i.e., originate interaction) to representatives of the material or maintenance departments. Any given interactional event was not likely to be dominated by one party or the other, as had been the case earlier; discussions were more reciprocal. Also, there was less tendency for those in production and those in the service groups to respond to differences of opinion by taking the problem through their formally separate channels for resolution at the top.

Individual and group interactions involving production supervision and those in departments with *control* functions, such as inspection and work standards, were distinctly altered by 1956. By the nature of its function, inspection was and continued to be the originator of many interactions directed

---

[10] All fifteen foremen who made specific comments about their contacts with these service groups reported this to be true.

at production supervision, but by 1956 inspection's function was no longer exclusively that of telling production supervision when the quality of work was unsatisfactory. Production foremen and general foremen observed in 1956 that "they got together much more often" with inspection supervision to clarify and to agree upon the meaning of inspection specifications. Knowing clearly what would "pass" or "not pass," foremen were able to halt "bad" jobs before they were passed on to later sections of the line, where "repair" would be much more difficult. Eliminating later repairs, and especially at points of "final" inspection, also reduced the necessity for those at later check points to initiate complaints back through earlier sections of the line. With less absenteeism and turnover of hourly workers and with more thorough training of new workers (foremen and their utility men had more time to work with the new men), the quality of output improved. This, in turn, reduced the necessity of inspection to interact with production.

As to another control group, the work standards department, in 1953 the determination of how much work a worker was to perform or how the several operations were to be distributed among a group of men under a foreman was often dictated by a representative of the work standards department. As it was often expressed, "They went strictly by the book." Interactions were originated primarily by work standards; the response was compliance or evasion by the foreman. By 1956 management altered work standards' role so that it came to accept a service as well as a control function. Foremen more frequently determined who was to do how much with respect to what job on the assembly line. In terms of interaction this meant fewer contacts were originated by work standards and directed at production supervision, and the proportion of contacts (not necessarily the total volume) made by the foreman to the work standards representative for technical advice was higher in 1956. As in many other events involving production and nonproduction groups, discussions between operating supervision and work standards were oriented more toward the future, that is, toward planning in advance for readjustments of work loads in light of a known schedule change to come.

Interactions between operating supervisors and the comptroller's office took on a completely different pattern by 1956. Previously there had been virtually no contact between the two. The accounting function had been primarily that of gathering cost data and of distributing standard reports to the internal organization and to the division. This primary reporting and controlling function had not changed by 1956, but the information was geared more closely to the requirements of the technical work flow and to the needs of supervision. Seen in interaction terms, what happened was that members of the comptroller's department, on the initiative of the plant manager, began to interact frequently with operating supervision. These interactions took place in paired events—between a representative of the comptroller's department and a line supervisor—as well as in set events at weekly cost meetings and group conferences. It became common practice for foremen and general foremen to go *to* the comptroller's department for information and for members of the comptroller's group to "go out on the floor." This was the pattern during 1954 and 1955. By 1956 detailed systems and procedures on cost data had become thoroughly routinized and accepted by production. The pattern of reciprocity continued when schedule changes were being discussed, but the gross rate of interaction was lower.

### 4. *Summary of Interaction Patterns*

An attempt has been made in this section to organize the qualitative material of the study in terms of a quantitative descriptive device, interaction. A general observation was made to the effect that, whereas no basic changes were made in the formal organization, there were substantial changes in the pattern of interactions among its members. In the former period a far greater proportion of interactions had been originated by superiors and directed to subordinates than was the case in the later period. In 1953 a superior's stimulus to act was most often based on *his* superior's action toward *him* and not on the advice or suggestions of his subordinate, as was more often the case in 1956. In events involving production supervisors and their peers in production and nonproduction departments the origin of interactions took on a more reciprocal pattern.

So much for *direction*: What about *frequency?* What can be said about gross differences in the total volume of interactions in 1956 when compared with 1953? We frankly cannot state as a fact that in one period it was greater or less than in the other period. Yet, the persistent and recurring theme in the interviews to the effect that members of Plant Y had "fewer emergencies and more time to plan" suggests that the total volume of interpersonal contacts *may have been considerably less* in 1956. For those who tend to correlate frequency of interaction and "group cohesiveness" the above observation raises some questions. The answers may be found when we consider more fully the technical as well as the social aspects of the total system.

For the balance of the present section we shall look at Plant Y in 1953 and in 1956 in terms of contrasting patterns of "sentiment" and, finally, in terms of measurable "performance" results.

## B. *SENTIMENTS*

The shift in the pattern of interactions among members of Plant Y from one period in time to another was accompanied by a change in the feelings that its members expressed toward one another. These expressed feelings will be labeled "sentiments," as defined and used by Homans.[11] The term represents something considerably less specialized than that found in the lexicon of psychology. Our purpose here is simply to look at the qualitative data presented earlier and to put forward what appear to be the major points of differences in sentiments.

---

[11] Homans, *op. cit.*, p. 37.

Sentiments were expressed about interpersonal relationships in general and about the behavior of one person to another in specific events. The earlier period had been marked by expressions of intense dissatisfaction at all levels. In the relationships of subordinates to superiors certain themes recurred. These were expressed as "fear," "confusion," "suspicion," and "pressure": for example, "This plant operates in a constant atmosphere of suspicion and pressure." Almost without exception the respondents deplored these conditions. Even the former manager, who was bitterly criticized by subordinates, admitted that he disliked having to deal autocratically with subordinates: "I can't treat my superintendents the way I get treated." But both he and his subordinates felt they had to conform to the pattern or lose their jobs even though "the system" was completely contrary to their basic feelings of "fair play." One of the general foremen, it is recalled, put it this way: "I began to believe that my whole thinking was wrong and that I should pattern myself after the way the people on top operated." Others frankly admitted that there was no alternative but to conform.

Subordinates repeatedly expressed to this observer ideas and suggestions as to what superiors should do to improve interpersonal relationships and technical operations. They said that their ability to communicate upward was blocked for many reasons, principal among them being emphasis on formal status and on the use of power inherent in each office.

"Those higher up never listen to us."
"The foremen are scared to make decisions."
"There is too much superiority in rank."
"This plant runs on fear alone."
"They just issue orders but don't understand the effects."
"They don't know how to get down to our level."

By 1956, expressions such as these were rare. All members accepted the same basic goals of production that they had before, but now they felt they were being motivated and were motivating others within an entirely different set of relationships.

"We still have pressure, but the pressure comes from us. It isn't based on fear."

"My boss listens to my ideas."

"Management expects me to run my section, but I get help when I ask for it."

"The boss treats me right because that's the way he is treated."

"It isn't perfect yet, but we're moving in the right direction."

There seemed to be little question in the minds of members of supervision that the behavior of the manager set the pattern from the day he took over. Nevertheless, it was only after subordinates saw action in the form of physical and organizational changes that their sentiments changed. The initial announcement by the manager that he did not believe in motivating people by threats and firings brought an immediate favorable response, but it was many months later (when the incumbents saw that there *were* no firings) before they came to believe what they had heard at first. "Action, not words, is what counts," is the way it was expressed.

In 1953 the source of expressed dissatisfaction had been as much "technical" as it was "personal." Most activity during the workday had centered on emergencies which stopped or threatened to stop the movement of the lines. "This place is just one damned emergency after another." Supervisors at all levels had complained (to this observer, but usually not to superiors) that they had no means of predicting possible breakdowns. They had attributed this condition to lack of information as to how their own individual operation fitted into the total picture. "We have to operate with departmental blinders on."

The favorable feelings expressed in 1956 may be attributed in part to the fact that *the members now saw much more of the total picture; their opinions were asked; they made suggestions.* They still had to obey orders in response to changing conditions brought about by outside forces, but since they now had a say in planning for change, they were much more willing to accept orders.

This shift in sentiments, they believed, came about not only through individual contacts, but by means of group meetings which increased in number and changed in content. The meetings in the early period had been looked upon as punishing, not rewarding experiences. "The manager just tries to put us on the spot." They reinforced what the participants had experienced with their own superiors in individual contacts on the shop floor. Meetings after 1953 were regarded as having a different kind of function. All present joined in attacking a technical problem. *The focus was on the problem, not on people.* That is, *individuals* were no longer singled out as scapegoats. Each member came to understand better the interrelationship of his own technical and social roles with those of others. "We came to look at the other guy's problems from *his* point of view." The manifest purpose of group meetings was to solve "business" problems, yet the experience of meeting as a group was meaningful in and of itself to the members.

The sentiments of those in production toward those responsible for service, control, and reporting functions changed rather remarkably. In both time periods members of operating supervision were held accountable for the efficiency of operations and for the quality of the product. In 1953, however, foremen had regarded the presence and actions of staff members with suspicion and resentment. The comptroller's efficiency figures had been used as a threat, not as an aid. The work standards representatives were believed to be "dictating" how the foremen should establish work loads. Foremen had come to feel that inspection's role was solely to "put us on the spot."

By 1956, with virtually no change in the functions of nonoperating groups as prescribed "in the manual," the roles of these groups were perceived quite differently and favorably. Those in the supporting groups were looked upon as agents for supplying information which was useful and helpful to the foremen for predictive purposes. Foremen felt that greater control was being given rather than being taken away from them.

The change in sentiments was not limited to a few people but, with only two exceptions, was generalized among all the members of the managerial staff from top to bottom. Some interviews were held with a superior and subordinate both of whom occupied the same positions in relation to one another in both periods. To hear what each said about the other in 1953 one would assume that the expressed antagonisms were functions of some basic "personality" differences. That such was not the case is revealed in the positive and favorable comments made in 1956. As one general foreman put it: "There are some people around here who I used to think were real bastards but they have changed a lot." *What seems to have happened is that conditions and relationship patterns had changed to such an extent that the members of the organization believed that the "personality" of a superior or subordinate had in fact changed.*

Here is an interesting and perhaps significant finding. This observer is not in a position to interpret these personality changes from the point of view of the clinical psychologist, but if they were as substantial as they appear to have been, the finding casts some doubt about the "constancy" of personality traits. Furthermore, one cannot avoid questioning the usefulness of many psychological tests as predictive devices when, as this study would indicate, prediction is so crucially dependent upon knowledge of the social and technical forces impinging on the individual at the time of the test.

The finding also has relevance to training. There is a basic assumption behind many "human relations" training programs throughout industry that it is possible to teach human relations "skills" apart from the socio-technical matrix in which such skills are to be exercised. The observation made here strongly suggests that "getting people to co-operate with one another" is not something that can be taught. A willingness to co-operate evolves from a change in the total system of relationships. It cannot be generated in the training classroom alone but must start at the top and permeate down through the entire organization in day-to-day relationships.[12]

---

[12] Further support for this assertion may be found in The Ohio State University studies. See especially E. A. Fleishman, W. E. Burtt, and E. F. Harris, *Leadership and Supervision in Industry: An Evaluation of a Supervisory Training Program.*

Is it possible, one might ask, that new kinds of negative sentiments emerged in the later period to replace the old? As far as could be determined none could be discerned. What dissatisfactions were expressed revolved around the theme of goal achievement. "We're going in the right direction but not fast enough."

If one were to make the most general kind of observation about the shift from one pattern of sentiments (negative) to another (positive), it would be this. Members of Plant Y adopted a mode of social behavior toward one another which more closely approximated the norms of behavior expected among friends and neighbors in the culture beyond the factory gates. At the same time this behavior, when it concerned the business at hand, was highly rational; it was as much problem oriented as it was person oriented.

With the present discussion of a marked shift in *sentiments* and an earlier description of an underlying shift in *interaction* patterns, it remains to discover whether the change in these two behavior elements bore any relationship to actual performance.

## C. *PERFORMANCE RESULTS*

Interpersonal contacts (interactions) and expressions of attitudes and feelings (sentiments) were related to the thousands of physical acts (activities) performed by members of Plant Y every day. The cumulative effect of these activities brought about certain *results* which could be measured according to indices of performance. The purpose of this summary section is to indicate the changes in performance that took place from 1953 to 1956. The data on performance include:

General efficiency (direct labor costs measured against standards)
Efficiency loss and recovery in periods of schedule change
Efficiency loss and recovery in periods of annual model change
Indirect labor costs
Quality performance
Safety record

Labor grievances
Absenteeism
Turnover

These measures, especially those of efficiency and quality, were generally regarded by all members of management at plant and corporate levels as the most important indices of performance. The first five are direct measures of organization performance. The last four are not measures of output as such, but the fact of a good or poor record in these categories can influence output substantially.

### 1. *General Efficiency*

It was observed earlier that in 1953 Plant Y required 16 per cent more direct labor to run the plant than was needed according to the standard of 100 per cent set by the division for all of is plants.[13] The next "poorest" performer measured 110 per cent: that is, it used 10 per cent more labor than was required by standards. (No plant among the six operated below 102 per cent.)

By 1956 Plant Y's direct labor costs had gone down 14 per cent. Its position was superior to that of any other plant in the division. Although no specific figures were available, a rough computation of average wages and total man hours indicates that a 14 per cent improvement represented a savings of more than $2 million in one year.

Graph I compares Plant Y with the other plants in both time periods.

### 2. *Efficiency Loss and Recovery in Periods of Schedule Change*

It is characteristic of every schedule change that labor costs rise precipitously for the first week after substantial increases or decreases in production are ordered. This is principally due to the fact that the work load of each of hundreds of line

---

[13] In 1953 there were six plants in the division. Later another plant was built. Some of the figures used in this section do not include the new plant.

GRAPH I
GENERAL EFFICIENCY—CHANGES IN DIRECT LABOR COSTS
FOR SIX PLANTS, 1953 AND 1956
(In Per Cent above 100% of Labor Standards)

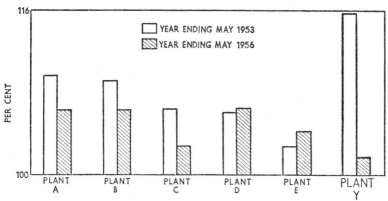

operations must be altered. The work of each operator must be rearranged to synchronize it with the speed of the conveyor. The ability of a plant to make a "quick recovery to normal" within three or four weeks can mean substantial savings, literally in hundreds of thousands of dollars. Recovery is generally regarded as a measure of administrative effectiveness.

In the 1953 period there had been a number of changes in production schedules which each plant had to face. The precise figures for this period were not available, but a senior staff member of the division reported that Plant Y's costs had risen higher than those of any other plant during major schedule changes and that its recovery had been slower.

In 1956 there were at least two major schedule changes affecting all plants. Both changes involved drastic cutbacks in production due to market conditions. Not only did Plant Y's costs rise *less* than did those of the other six plants, but it "recovered" more quickly than any of the others.

Graph II plots the losses for each plant for each of two schedule changes beginning with the week before the production cutback and continuing to the fourth week after the cutback.

GRAPH II
EFFICIENCY LOSSES AND RECOVERY IN TWO PERIODS OF SCHEDULE
CHANGES DURING 1956—SEVEN PLANTS COMPARED
(In Per Cent above 100% of Labor Standards)

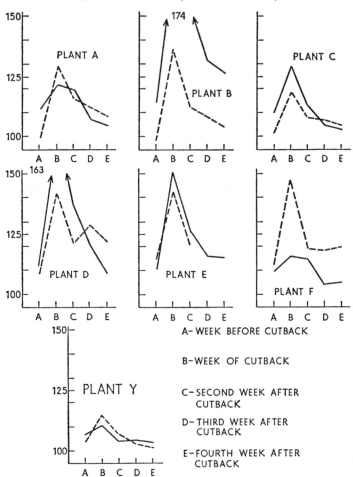

## 3. *Efficiency Loss and Recovery in Periods of Model Change*

The introduction of new models is the industry's "annual headache" from a production standpoint. As in the case of schedule changes, each plant tries to reach the required line speed as quickly as possible and at the least possible cost.

In the fall of 1956 (introducing the 1957 car models), Plant Y came up to line speed more quickly than did any of the other six plants. Also, during the three months following the introduction of new models total manufacturing costs were 15 *per cent less* than those of the next best performer and 50 *per cent lower* than the poorest among the seven plants.

### 4. *Indirect Labor Costs*

The costs of operating the various nonproduction departments, relative to the estimated cost of each car unit produced, had been higher in 1953 at Plant Y than it had been for any of the other plants in the division. A breakdown for nonproduction departments for 1956 was available only for the "material and production control" department. By September, 1956, the average cost per unit for this department had been reduced to the point where it shared the best position with one other plant in the division.

### 5. *Quality Performance*

The staff head of quality control for the division stated that Plant Y's position in 1953 could not be compared precisely with that of other plants, "but it was certainly one of the poorest." By January, 1956, it moved up to third place and for the balance of the year consistently held either top or second position in the division.

### 6. *Safety Performance*

In its monthly safety record (lost-time accidents) Plant Y had been fourth, fifth, or last place most of the time among the division's plants in 1953. In 1955 its position had begun to improve slightly, but by 1956, and during each month from January to June of that year, it maintained top position in the division. In fact, during May, 1956, it stood fourth among more than 126 plants in the entire corporation, a remarkable feat considering that the potential for accidents was clearly higher than it was for many other types of production operations.

### 7. *Labor Grievances*

As Graph III indicates, Plant Y had the second highest record number of formal labor grievances per month per 100 employees in 1953. In the twelve months prior to June, 1956, not only had the average number of grievances per month been reduced, but its record, as shown in Graph III, was substantially better than that of any of the other six plants in the division.

GRAPH III

AVERAGE NUMBER OF GRIEVANCES PER 100 WORKERS, 1953 AND 1956
(Based on Monthly Averages for Seven Plants)

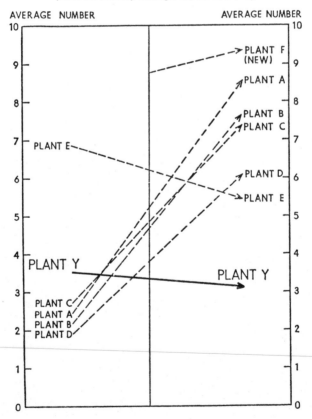

### 8. *Absenteeism*

Plant Y's absentee rate (short-term personal absenteeism measured as a percentage of scheduled work) dropped from 4.1 per cent in 1953 to 2.5 per cent in 1956.

### 9. *Turnover*

Plant Y's average monthly rate of turnover among hourly workers dropped from 6.1 per cent in 1953 to 4.9 per cent in 1956.

### 10. *Summary of Performance*

Considering the basic purpose of Plant Y as a production organization the evidence is overwhelming that a sharp, dramatic change took place when one compares the two time periods. Not only was there a substantial improvement noticeable when Plant Y's performance was measured against itself, but its performance, when compared with five (later six) other similar assembly plants, went from bottom to top position in most indices of performance. These comparative data are important as proof that the improvement was something generated internally inasmuch as *all* plants were subject to the same external market conditions. All were similar in product, technology, and formal structure of organization. All managers reported to the same divisional manager. In short, the performance change which took place in this organization over the span of three years can hardly be explained on the basis of chance.

## D. *CONCLUDING REMARKS ABOUT INTERACTION, SENTIMENTS, AND PERFORMANCE*

The purpose of this chapter has been to compare the organization in two periods of time using three elements of behavior as a descriptive framework. Two distinct patterns were observed. Plant Y as a "system state" in Time I when contrasted with Time II was characterized by a communications system in which a high proportion of interactions were originated by superiors to subordinates. Expressed sentiments about one's relationship to others and about conditions in general were extremely negative. Performance was inferior both when compared with Plant Y's later performance and when contrasted with the performance of other similar plants. Time II was marked by a greater "balance" in interactions between levels and functions, highly favorable sentiments, and superior performance.

This observation supports in part Homans' hypotheses about small group behavior, except that it can now be stated so as to include the "product" of a given interaction-sentiment pattern. Thus, to the extent that interactions between persons at various levels of a complex hierarchical group are originated by superiors or by members of one specialized group to others, sentiments of tension and hostility will be high and performance will be low.

Stated in this way this hypothesis oversimplifies an extremely complex set of conditions and relationships. Nevertheless, it may be regarded as a first step—a way of handling qualitative data in a more quantitative manner. For example, Gouldner describes "punishment-centered" versus "representative" behavior in bureaucratic organizations and in a general way links this behavior to expressed feelings of the members and by inference, to performance. In many other studies (mostly in small groups) patterns of communication are linked to attitudes and feelings but only occasionally, to performance.[14]

When it comes to understanding behavior in complex organizations, the "evidence" linking a pattern of communications to "morale" is frequently stated in qualitative form. Subordinates express *hostility* to a *directive* or *authoritarian* pattern of communications. The assumption is then made that such conditions must lead to poor performance results.

---

[14] L. Coch and J. R. P. French, Jr., "Overcoming Resistance to Change," *Human Relations*, Vol. I, No. 4 (August, 1948), pp. 512–32.

What is being suggested here is that qualitative labels need to be and can be made more precise; they can be quantified. Interactions can be counted. The pattern of who originates action for whom can be observed (or extrapolated from interviews) and the direction determined. Expressed feelings or sentiments can be identified as being on the positive or negative side of a continuum. In the present study it was easy to place the sentiment pattern at two extremes in Time I and Time II. Performance results, by definition, are quantitative data. The researcher's practical problem is how to get at these data.

As more sophisticated quantitative tools of description are devised, it will become easier to find common ground for comparing many types of production organizations. Or, as was done in this study, the same organization can be described at two separate intervals in time. If it is found that a given interaction-sentiment pattern can be associated with certain predicted performance results, this kind of finding should be important to practitioner and theorist.

The comparative approach is useful but somewhat limited. It is useful for comparing two system states. We can learn something about the social processes which apparently lead to success or failure. Such comparisons, however, are essentially static; they fail to explain "process" in the larger temporal sense, that is, *the process by which a complex system changes from one state to another following the introduction of some agent of change.* This larger change process is the focus of the next chapter.

# CHAPTER 7

# The Process of Change

The purpose of this section is to look again at the descriptive material in the study in order to understand more clearly how a complex socio-technical system such as Plant Y evolves from one state to another over time. In discussing the change process a certain amount of arbitrary structuring will be necessary. That is, change will be discussed in terms of phases, as if one phase in the change process followed another in a distinct time sequence. Actually, the phases often overlapped one another, and in some instances the pattern of events starting up in one phase continued through several subsequent phases.

## A. CRITICAL CONDITIONS LEADING TO THE FIRST PHASE OF CHANGE

The condition which ultimately forced action and which set in motion a complex sequence of events leading to change was Plant Y's continued failure to perform according to the requirements established by the division and corporation. This condition, as we have seen, had brought about a division-to-plant relationship marked by frequent downward-directed interaction. The division, to an increasing extent, had used explicit or implied threats of reprisal against members of Plant Y and especially against the manager. The manager had reacted to these threats by transmitting the division's orders to subordinates. He had rarely taken the initiative to persuade the division to modify its orders. In addition to the directives aimed specifically at Plant Y, there were general directives to all plants ordering production increases or cutbacks. For

Plant Y such alterations in line speeds only exacerbated the existing socio-technical problems.

Those immediately under the manager, preoccupied with their own job survival, had received directives and had transmitted them to their subordinates, and so on down to the lowest levels. Each new directive had reinforced the prevailing sentiments of fear and anxiety. Actions were limited primarily to carrying out directives and to correcting immediate technical difficulties. As these technical difficulties increased (because the basic interactional system hindered permanent solutions), over-all productivity of the organization decreased, and this in turn brought on further directives from above.

In one sense these conditions represent a classical example of Merton's "dysfunction." However, Merton stated that the tensions and strains "may be instrumental in leading to changes in the system,"[1] implying that the organizational unit itself would somehow change internally so as to reduce tension and achieve its rational objectives. The same notion of internal "readjustment" is put forward by Homans, Bakke, and others who talk about "equilibrium." Haire hypothesizes "that the organization will grow strongest when the forces tending to destroy it are strongest."[2]

This study suggests that a point may be reached *when an organization is not capable of changing itself internally.* The spiraling effect of superior-originated interactions, of increased tension, and of low performance may be broken only by action of some agent outside the immediate organization. This is what happened at Plant Y when the division retired the manager and installed another.

## B. *PHASES IN THE CHANGE PROCESS*

### 1. *The Succession of a New Manager*

The events of the first few days may be regarded as a crucial phase in the change process at Plant Y. At least the members

---

[1] Robert K. Merton, *Social Theory and Social Structure,* p. 123.
[2] Mason Haire, *Modern Organization Theory,* p. 11.

of the organization perceived these events as something more than the "arrival of another boss." His initial acts—where he sat at the introductory dinner, to whom he talked, how he dressed, and especially what he said—impressed the group. By publicly disclaiming any intention to use punishment as a means for getting action he touched on a basic need—the need for job security. Some changes in sentiments may be said to have taken place in the organization at this point; members now expressed the hope that the manager was not going to rely on the punitive powers of his office to influence behavior.

There was one significant change, not in the organization itself, but in its relationship to the division. From the day of the new manager's arrival there was an abrupt reduction of "interference from above." Standard directives, notices, and information of the kind all plants received continued, but specific directives—ordering the manager at Plant Y what to do in response to each administrative crisis—came to a halt. Curiously enough, the division manager's expectations of the new manager had not substantially changed at the time of succession. The new manager was expected to use the power of his office to "clean house" and replace many members of the subordinate organization. Yet as events later showed, this was not done, and the division manager never insisted that it should be. This shift in "pressure" from the division cannot be explained by any sudden improvement in the plant's performance results. There was no immediate improvement. What appears to have happened (and this is admittedly speculative based on a single comment of a high corporation official) was that the division manager himself was urged by superiors to allow the new plant manager considerable latitude in "running his own show." Top management added a "blank check" clause in their instructions to the manager, "We don't care what you do as long as you get the plant out of the mess it is in." This is what the manager "heard," and he took full advantage of it.

## 2. *The Manager's Becoming Informed about the Needs of the Organization*

There is substantial agreement in the literature to the effect that the leader of a group must have a realistic understanding of the needs of his "followers" in order to change their behavior. He must be "in tune with" the group's needs. Learning about these needs is clearly one of the early phases in successful organizational change under new leadership. Not much is known about the *process* by which a new leader learns about these needs.

The new manager at Plant Y, beginning the first day in the plant, chose the most direct means he could to learn about the needs of the organization as seen by its members. As described earlier, he went out into the plant and talked with several people from his immediate staff down to the workers.

In this phase interactions were originated almost entirely by the manager. Once the interactions were initiated, however, members were urged to "freewheel" on problems that they thought needed attention. Here was a significant shift in the content of interactions between manager and subordinates. Subordinates perceived the manager's conversations not as preludes to directives by the manager, as had been the case before, but as an informal means for them to comment on problems and solutions as seen by the subordinates. This was looked upon as a first step in opening up the channels of information to higher echelons.

This early informal and random interactional mechanism brought about little change in the day-to-day activities of the members of Plant Y. It is worth repeating that there was no sudden improvement in performance. At best, the effect of the manager's behavior was to reinforce favorable sentiments of individuals toward the manager, feelings and opinions which had begun to change as a result of his introductory statements. Even the many persons who had not met the manager face to face were, during the first few months, beginning to "get the word through the grapevine." These random contacts "out on the floor" helped the manager to accumulate technical information and to acquire knowledge about the needs of subordinates which served to guide his future actions.

### 3. "Institutionalizing" Interactions

For a new pattern of behavior to become established and enlarged to cover all segments of an organization, something more is necessary than a shift in the relationship between single individuals and the head of the organization. Ways must be found to "institutionalize" the basic sentiment-interaction pattern so that it is no longer random or fortuitous behavior involving one man and more than 300 supervisory subordinates (and three to five thousand persons under them).

The establishment of the various types of regularly scheduled meetings between the manager and those in the upper echelons introduced a systematic exchange of information among the various functional heads of the organization.

Those participating gained further assurance that the new manager was not using and did not intend to use autocratic measures to gain acceptance. Participants freely expressed ideas and suggestions not only to the manager but, what is perhaps even more important, to one another. The meetings introduced a new form of lateral or peer interaction among those in the higher echelons which was sustained not in the meetings alone but in day-to-day relationships. Thus, one segment of the total organization—members at higher levels—had within the first few months adopted a pattern of interpersonal relationships which later spread to all levels of the managerial group. How persons behaved in the group meetings and how this behavior was adopted by others so that it later became "routine" throughout all levels we have identified as an "institutionalizing" process.

Also, during this early phase certain physical changes were made as a result of the discussions. These changes were designed to improve working conditions, not to increase productivity directly. Such innovations in the physical environment served as visual and concrete evidence to those at lower levels that upper management "meant what it said" about making changes. These improvements had a generalized effect on sentiments even though the day-to-day relationships at lower levels do not appear to have changed substantially up to this point in time (approximately six months). In other words, for them the basic pattern of interactions had not yet become institutionalized as it had for the top staff. Nevertheless, with this concrete evidence of change, they were better prepared psychologically to respond favorably to the new pattern which was slowly permeating down from above.

### 4. Enlarging the Span of Cognition

A characteristic of all bureaucratic organizations is the specialization of functions. In the present study it was observed that conflicts often arose because one individual or group had little understanding of how his own actions affected and were affected by the actions of those performing other functions. Factual information about over-all operations was either withheld, was inaccurate, or was lacking altogether. At some point in the change process there evolved a greater awareness of, knowledge about, and an active interest in the role which others were performing and which gave greater meaning to their own specialized task. This is essentially a rational or cognitive process, hence the term broadening or enlarging one's "span of cognition."

With an increase in reciprocal interactions (as contrasted with unidirectional contacts) between the manager and others and across departmental lines—a result, in part, of the system of meetings—a greater awareness of how the total organization "fitted together" began to emerge. On the cognitive level members were not only learning what was going on in other areas of the immediate organization, but they were receiving more advance information about divisional activities and decisions which would affect them in the future.

Enlarging an individual's span of cognition was no longer

limited to staff heads. Those at lower levels were to an increasing extent "getting together," as they worded it, in pairs and in groups to share new ideas. The several permanent position shifts vertically and laterally and the temporary assignments to higher jobs also served to broaden each man's understanding of the relation of the parts to the whole. It might be pointed out parenthetically that the manager himself was subject to this same process of enlargement. He did not enter the scene with full knowledge of what Plant Y's problems were, nor did he come in with elaborate preformulated ideas as to what needed to be done to solve them.

By the end of the first year the basic pattern of interpersonal relationships was set (positive sentiments and reciprocal interactions); it remained to make the technical moves to improve performance.

### 5. *Planning and Action*

The phases through which Plant Y had passed thus far led to a consensus on what specific technological innovations and administrative actions were necessary to raise the over-all productivity of the organization. Agreements were reached on priorities. A characteristic of this phase was the tendency for decisions and actions to be taken not only by the manager and his staff, but by those at lower levels as well. On major matters the organization had to obtain support and approval of the parent organization. Here the manager played an increasingly important role in gaining divisional support. Unlike the previous manager, he was "armed" with realistic information as to the organization's needs. Not having to act primarily out of fear of punishment he was able to ask for and receive financial and other support.

Decisions which were followed by orders to act met virtually no resistance from subordinate groups since it was apparent to them that they had had a part in planning for the action taken. Recommendations which foremen, inspection supervisors, plant engineering personnel and scores of other supervisors had made began to be translated into concrete changes in the technical system. At the end of the new manager's first two years at the plant, performance results began to show some signs of improvement.

### 6. *Reinforcement of Results*

After two and one-half years the results of the several technical and administrative actions were evident. Each new announcement showing that the plant was overtaking other plants in the several performance indices reinforced the members' confidence in their ability to change. There was now what Arensberg calls a "high degree of convergence" between the goals or values of the manager and of those in the subordinate managerial group.

Perhaps the most distinctive feature of this reinforcement phase was that stopgap emergency measures for coping with new problems were virtually eliminated. In the previous phases planning had taken place under conditions still marked by many technical and communication breakdowns. Now the availability of time for planning purposes increased cumulatively. Members had more time to take care of their own work and more time to interact with others outside of their own area.

To authorities above the plant level, performance results were the most important criteria against which the plant was judged. Plant Y was now moving up to the position of the leader in the division. The plant's new favorable position made it still easier for plant management to argue successfully for financial support of technical improvements.

Thus there was a spiraling effect in precisely the opposite direction from that at the time preceding the succession of the new manager. Under the former manager, each action or set of events had tended to make it increasingly difficult, if not impossible, for the organization to improve performance and to readjust itself internally; it had gone beyond the "point of no return." By the last phase of the new administration, the ability to change and to adjust had become "built into" the organization. Now each action or set of events over time made it increasingly *possible* to make internal adjustments to new external conditions.

A central question remains: What would happen if the man who originally triggered the change process should leave the organization? Or put another way, to what extent does continued success depend upon the actions and influence of the manager?

### 7. Final Phase—Aftermath

At the end of three years the "new" manager left Plant Y. He was promoted to a higher position in the division. For the next two years Plant Y not only maintained itself as the leader of the seven plants in the division, but its performance, as measured by all indices, was better than it had been before. The groundwork had been laid earlier. The system was geared to meet changing external conditions; it was capable of generating *new* ideas for improvement. The fact of continued improvement makes it clear that once a pattern of relationships has been found rewarding and productive, an organization does not have to depend on any unique actions of its leader to sustain its success.

## C. OBSERVATIONS

The present study points to a number of propositions or hypotheses about the change process in complex organizations. A single case study cannot "prove" that all organizations moving from a state of dysfunction to efficiency necessarily pass through phases similar to this one. And yet it is quite possible that under conditions generally similar to those reported here one might be able to discern a basic pattern of changing behavior over time which would yield similar results in other formal organizations. Those doing further research on theories of organization change might consider the following:

*Observation No. 1*

When an organization is a subordinate unit to a larger organization, and when the patterns of internal relationships within the subordinate organization are similar to those linking it to the larger, changes leading to more successful performance within the subordinate organization will take place *after* there has been a change in the pattern of relationships (interactions and sentiments) linking the larger to the subordinate organization.

This observation comes from the record of this industrial plant's relationship to the division and corporation. Here it was noted that in Period I of the study, before the installation of a new manager, nothing done internally had any effect in reducing conflict and in improving performance. If anything, performance and "morale" continued to deteriorate. This trend was arrested not only by the actions of a new manager but also by a change in the division's behavior toward the plant. There was less immediate direction of the plant's activities (reduction in the proportion of interactions originated by the division) and a change in the division's attitude toward the plant manager. Threats of punishment were replaced by expressions of confidence and support.

This same observation about the relationship of the subordinate organization toward the larger may also be applied to the relationships linking superiors and subordinates within the subordinate (plant) organization itself. That is, more reciprocal interaction between subordinates and superiors, the elimination of fear, and an increase in favorable sentiments mutually expressed by superiors and subordinates toward one another came about at lower levels only *after* there was a change in the basic behavior linking middle and lower supervision to the manager and members of the top staff. When this took place performance began to improve.

*Observation No. 2*

The length of time required for an organization to improve its performance results is a function of:

*a*) The size of the organization in terms of the number of individuals.

*b*) The number of levels in the hierarchy.

*c*) The number of specialized service, reporting, and control groups.

*d*) The complexity of technical operations.

*e*) The degree of intensity of personal insecurity and of inter-personal hostility at the outset of the change process.

In the present study the elapsed time before any substantial results became evident was two and one-half years. It is quite possible that changes would have taken place more quickly in a smaller, less complex organization. Only further research in a variety of organizations undergoing change can support this assertion.

### Observation No. 3

For a complex organization to move from one pattern of behavior to another it is *not* necessary that its formal structure be altered.

Despite the several innovations and changes which were made in this organization nothing was done to alter its form as symbolized in the chart of organization. The number of levels, the number of subordinates reporting to superiors on each level, the number and types of line and staff groups, the descriptions of the purposes and responsibilities of the departments and of each managerial position in each department—none of these changed. Nor was there any major change in the written rules and regulations established by the division or corporation which defined both generally and specifically what the plant could or could not do.

This observation has some interesting practical as well as theoretical implications. From experience in many types of industrial organizations this researcher has been struck by the frequency with which executives and managers attempt to improve the performance of an organization simply by altering its structural or "legal" form. Departments are split up or combined. Levels are eliminated "to assure more direct communications and control." Functions are integrated horizontally (all functions under one command) or vertically (each function reporting up through separate commands). Undoubtedly, such alterations can change the entire system of interpersonal relations leading to measurable performance changes. The question this study raises is whether such structural manipulations are always necessary. If our hypothesis is correct it suggests that before shifting functions and levels on an organization chart, those in command positions might do well to consider more carefully the organization's performance potential under the existing structure.

### Observation No. 4

The process of successful change in a hierarchical organization will start and continue to the extent that the members perceive the behavior of superiors, peers, and subordinates to be more in keeping with the norms of behavior in the larger culture.

In some respects this hypothesis falls more appropriately in the next section. Here it may be observed that behavior was judged as legitimate not only on a utilitarian basis, that is, whether it would help production, but also on the basis of whether it was "democratic." The rules of conduct appropriate to friends and neighbors and to members of a culture with a strong egalitarian tradition were frequently cited as the criteria of legitimate in-plant behavior. Such rules were violated in the first period and "lived up to" in the later period. Not only did the members believe this to be true, but the fundamental pattern of more balanced interactions, eventually carried through to all levels of the managerial group, confirmed it. An important dimension of the change process was this growing awareness that in-plant relationships were becoming more consistent with those which the members experienced, or at least hoped to experience, outside the plant.

# CHAPTER 8

# The Nature of Authority in Perspective

## A. *THE PROBLEM OF DEFINING AUTHORITY AND DETERMINING ITS DERIVATION*

Stewart and Cooley, predecessor and successor, both "possessed" the formal authority to run the organization. What was the nature of this authority that made one fail and the other succeed?

Except for some references to the literature on organization and leadership in earlier sections little has been said about the nature of authority. Thus far, the only observation has been that "authority based upon fear of punishment was transferred into authority based upon acceptance and reward." Bennis has defined authority as "the process by which an agent induces a subordinate to behave in a desired manner." [1] While accepting this definition tentatively, the term "authority" has a more specialized meaning than the broader term "power," which might also be applied to Bennis' definition. Authority has the connotation of legality or of legitimacy. The institution of which the inducing agent is a member has established prescribed boundaries within which the agent can act. In the present study both managers (the "agents") acted within prescribed boundaries but played different roles and with different results. Here we are concerned with the way authority was exercised by the new manager inasmuch as it was his suc-

---

[1] Warren G. Bennis, "Leadership Theory and Administrative Behavior," *Administrative Science Quarterly*, Vol. 4, No. 3 (December, 1959), p. 295.

cession, not any other new factors introduced, which triggered the changes to follow. If one accepts the above definition of authority as a point of departure, it is necessary to "move the case" to a more abstract frame of reference and to see where it supports or modifies what others have said about the nature of authority.

The problem of defining authority has been difficult for many reasons. People have tried to generalize about it only to find that such generalizations differ radically depending upon the type of group or organization being described. Also, there is difficulty in reconciling the viewpoints of the rational or "classical" organization theorists, the "human relations" school, and the "revisionists" who try to combine elements of both.

Practical experience combined with a measure of sophisticated research in industrial organization has led us to discard the extreme explanations to the effect that authority is derived *solely* from (*a*) power vested in the office by higher "authorities" or from (*b*) power granted only by approval of subordinates or from (*c*) the influence of unique charismatic traits of the leader. Discarding extreme positions, however, has only partially clarified the question of why some leaders exercise authority successfully and others do not. Criteria used to measure effective authority have differed from study to study. Some investigators have measured leadership characteristics against effects on attitudes and satisfactions of subordinates.[2] Others have talked about the leader's authority stemming from his ability to help others toward "self-actualization."[3] Still others have used productivity as a measurement of effective authority.[4] In the present study the ultimate measurement has been performance.

Apart from the problem of criteria there is the question as to what kinds of group or organizational conditions are as-

---

[2] Charles R. Walker, Robert H. Guest, and Arthur N. Turner, *The Foremen on the Assembly Line.*

[3] Chris Argyris, *Personality and Organization.*

[4] Rensis Likert, "Developing Patterns in Management," *General Management Series No. 78,* American Management Association, 1955.

sociated with a given authority pattern. Authority appears to manifest itself quite differently depending upon whether one is talking about the leader of a street-corner gang, a chairman of the board of aldermen, the deacon in a church, or the student who is chosen by the group in a controlled laboratory situation. Finally, there are broad differences between cultures. The authority exercised by a successful assembly plant manager in Red China is probably quite different from that exercised by the successful manager at Plant Y.

Certain common themes about organization and the role of the leader emerge from what may be called the "classical" (Bennis)[5] or "rational" (Gouldner)[6] streams of thought exemplified by Weber, or by Taylor and those representing the "scientific management" school. In general these observers, imbued with the scientific determinism of the preceding century, held that the agent of authority was able to command obedience on the basis of power vested in him by those outside the organization. For Weber, it was society which legitimatized the exercise of authority. For the scientific management group, authority was something which could be built into the system much as one determines what sources of power are to be used in running machines. For Taylor, science dictated the design of organization and with it the design of a leader's authority. All stressed the importance of rationality and predictability. Only if those designing and running an organization based their actions on rationally measurable grounds could the authority they exercised yield the desired results.

As will be pointed out later the present study does not dismiss the contributions of these observers. The successful leader in the case of Plant Y was initially put in the position by agents *outside* of the immediate organization; he was not chosen by the group. Furthermore, rationality and predictability were central to interpreting performance results under his direction.

---

[5] Bennis, *op. cit.*, p. 261.

[6] Alvin W. Gouldner, "Organizational Analysis," in Robert K. Merton, Leonard Broom, and Leonard S. Cottrell, Jr. (eds.), *Sociology Today—Problems and Prospects*, p. 401.

We turn now to those who explain the source of leadership authority in the context of what Gouldner calls the "natural system"[7] model or what has been loosely called the "human relations" approach to organization. In the industrial sphere this stream of thought and its many tributaries assumed that a leader can best exercise authority by acting on the basis of the socio-psychological needs of his subordinates. Authority is derived from the group,[8] or is the "right to make decisions which are accepted" (Suojanen).[9] Gouldner called it the "representative bureaucratic" mode of authority.[10] Those interested in organizational therapy, such as Carl Rogers and Thomas Gordon, said that the successful leader exercises authority with the primary concern for "facilitating the group's development . . . aiding the group to actuate itself."[11] Moreno implied that authority was linked to affective preferences or sociometric choice.[12] The followers of Lewin have generally held that authority is conferred by the group on that person who can best meet its needs.[13]

It may be unfair to group these several streams of thought together, but there are some common denominators which clearly distinguish them from the classical or rational ways of looking at authority.[14]

Recent efforts have been made by some of the students cited above and by others to reconcile the classical and natural system points of view. (This study itself attempts to reconcile elements of both.) How a person "induced others to act in a desired direction" is seen to be not a function of membership consent alone. The leader is something more than a person who reacts solely on the basis of needs of the subordinates. Status

---

[7] *Ibid.*, p. 405.

[8] Robert K. Merton, *Social Theory and Social Structure*, p. 340.

[9] Waino W. Suojanen, "Leadership, Authority and Span of Control," *Advanced Management*, Vol. 22, No. 9 (September, 1957), p. 18.

[10] Alvin W. Gouldner, *Patterns of Industrial Bureaucracy*, p. 24.

[11] Carl Rogers, *Client-Centered Therapy*, p. 336.

[12] Jacob L. Moreno, *Who Shall Survive?* (rev. ed.).

[13] T. Main and W. Nysander, "Some Observations on Training-Groups," unpublished manuscript, Bethel, Maine, 1951, cited by W. G. Bennis, *op. cit.*, p. 271.

[14] Bennis, *op. cit.*, p. 272.

and power differentials conferred by those other than subordinates are important. Economic conditions and technical factors external to interpersonal relationships have a very real conditioning effect on the manner in which a leader can induce others to act. Cognition, rationality, prediction, and many of the behavior elements first recognized by Weber and others are now again being considered in attempts to determine the source of authority. What was perhaps most disturbing among those who sought to relate types of leadership patterns to group behavior was that *results* of behavior, using productivity as the criterion, did not prove that one method of exercising authority was necessarily more successful than any other method. In the present study we have at least been able to introduce tangible performance data.

Douglas McGregor has recently come forth with an approach to reconciling the two general streams of thought.[15] Some of his observations are appropriate in explaining the derivation of authority in the present study. McGregor wholly accepts the fact that there is inherent tension between the leader's attempt to exercise authority as an agent of "still higher authorities" (in the present case, the division and corporation) and his efforts to find out about and act upon the needs of subordinates. McGregor emphasizes first that the prerogatives of power come about not simply through incumbency of office nor from consent by subordinates but by a *collaborative process of goal attainment*. Success may be achieved when the job requirements of leader and followers are "set by the *situation;* they need not be seen by either party as personal requirements established by the superior." [16] As an illustration it may be recalled that in the present study, under the former manager, subordinates had felt they *had* to act not on the basis of rational technical problems but on the basis of their perception of what they thought the manager personally wanted, and he acted similarly toward his divisional superiors. The new manager and his subordinates focused their attention on technical problems. The manager's authority stemmed

---

[15] Douglas McGregor, "Notes on Organization Theory."
[16] *Ibid.,* p. 2.

from the kinds of contributions he was in a position to make in solving these problems. Subordinates did not feel they had to respond solely because he was the "boss." Both he and they responded to a *"situation."*

A second principle of McGregor's stemming from the first is that of *interdependence.* Successful exercise of authority requires not only a recognized dependence on the part of subordinates but a reciprocal and acknowledged recognition of the leader's dependence on subordinates. McGregor explained this principle in psychological terms; in the present study we have described it in terms of manifest behavior. The new leader openly acknowledged his dependence on his subordinates. Interactionally it has been described simply as a greater balance in the origination of interactions.

Another principle McGregor calls *"integration."* In describing this principle, McGregor points out that the acknowledgment of interdependence, referred to above, may bring about greater mutual confidence between leader and subordinates, but that satisfaction stemming from this does not necessarily bring about better performance results. A "happy ship," naval tradition notwithstanding, is not always a "taut ship." By emphasizing "target setting" McGregor indicates that a leader gains his power when he "can create conditions such that his subordinates perceive that they will satisfy their own needs and achieve their own purpose best by working toward organization objectives."[17] This is what he means by *integration.* He is suggesting that many of the subordinates' needs *as they perceive them* are often precisely the same as those of top management—the need to see to it that the technical system runs efficiently.

There is much in the present study to support this observation. When we look closely at what members of Plant Y said they wanted, it was not only a reduction of interpersonal conflict and the elimination of fear as such; a primary need, at least while they worked in the plant, was to have the *technical system function efficiently.* The former manager wanted effi-

---

[17] *Ibid.*, pp. 12–13.

ciency as much as subordinates did, if not more so, but he could not induce them to work for the objectives of the organization as a whole when he did little to help individuals achieve the production objectives of their immediate departments. The new manager in a very real sense "integrated" the larger with the immediate objectives and in so doing helped the supervisors do what they had always wanted to do but couldn't —run their own operations efficiently. It is worth repeating that the reduction of interpersonal conflict depended upon and emerged concurrently with improvements in the technical system.

Although he never specifically spelled out the implications of his principles for the problem of authority in a given industrial context, McGregor seemed to be implying that a successful leader's authority to induce others to act is derived from the successful "juggling" of a dual role which he must play. He is an agent of the power which others higher in the organization have vested in the office he holds and which subordinates accept (Weber described this role long ago). He is also an agent of the power which those in the immediate organization have vested in him because of what he can do *for them*.

Gouldner has made a substantial contribution to the dual-role theory of leadership in complex organizations. He clearly saw the necessity for reconciling what he calls the "rational system model of organization" and the "natural system model." On the matter of authority he says that two kinds of authority are legitimatized simultaneously in the same organization.[18] One kind is based upon the power of office formally vested in a head of an organization by higher authorities. The other kind of authority is based on "expertise." The latter, Gouldner holds, is something more than superior technical knowledge; it includes administrative skills, and central to these skills is the ability of the leader to act with sensitivity toward the needs of subordinates. The successful leader, Gouldner implies, must carry out two different roles if the organization is to be productive.

---

[18] Gouldner, *op. cit.*, "Organizational Analysis," p. 413.

How the successful manager at Plant Y carried out this dual role can be shown as one looks at the sequence of events preceding, during, and following a major decision by the manager. For example, he saw that a given section or department was faced with a concrete technical problem. The ultimate solution involved the expenditure of funds, a decision which the division would have to make. The manager's role was to encourage subordinates to work out the details of the solution. In this process, he acted as a consultant and helper without dictating the solution. Using what was primarily the subordinates' solution to their problem he "represented" them to higher management. Once he secured approval his role became one of ordering that the plan be carried out in much the same way that any head of an organization would issue an order. For the subordinate group to respect the manager's authority and to take effective action after the order was issued required that he first perform the initial or what Gouldner might call the "representative" role.

Before proceeding one must come to grips with a question about the leader's authority which this observer may have dismissed too lightly. The question is: Is it not so that the new manager's personality, intelligence, and knowledge were the crucial factors in explaining why he was able to exercise his authority succesfully? The answer is, "yes, partially." Certainly members of the organization spoke of him as the "kind of person who inspires confidence." His speech, dress, and actions were often contrasted with those of his predecessor. Just how different the two men were in terms of internal adjustment or of neurotic tendencies is not known inasmuch as we did not have the benefit of clinical observation by a trained clinical psychologist. Whether such information about "internal states" would have altered the general conclusion is a question. Our concern all the way through has been with overt behavior and with patterns of relationships in a complex socio-technical system. This is essentially a sociological study: our interest has been focused on the *situation*. The main business, as Gouldner would put it, has been "the analysis of a specific bureaucracy as a complex social system, concerned less with the individual differences of the actors than with the situationally shaped roles they perform."[19] As one example, it is highly unlikely that the new manager, whatever his personality characteristics may have been, would have been able to exercise authority over his subordinates as he did if the basic pattern of "pressure" from the division had persisted. A change in the external situation allowed the new manager to perform the role he did.

As to the matter of differences in intelligence and operating experience (what Weber described as authority based upon "expertise"), there is no evidence to indicate that the new manager had any advantage over the old. In fact, the former manager Stewart had had a longer and broader range of successful managerial experience than had Cooley. Also, comments about the former manager were often heard in 1953 such as "I'll give him credit for being a damn smart operator," or "He knows the car business cold." The new manager, as was pointed out, did not enter the scene with any specific substantive information as to how the physical operations could be improved. He learned this only after a more superior "idea-collecting" mechanism had formed within the total organization.

Finally, if personality, intelligence, and experience of one person are used as the primary arguments for explaining Plant Y's success it leaves unanswered the question as to why the organization continued to improve long after the new manager left.

We can now summarize those definitions and observations about the nature of authority that appear to be supported by the present study. Following this we will attempt to introduce additional insights which have not been elaborated in previous studies.

The process by which an agent induces subordinates to act in a desired manner varies according to the type of organiza-

---

[19] Gouldner, *op. cit.*, *Patterns of Industrial Bureaucracy*, p. 3.

tion being considered. In the present case, the organization had the following characteristics:

1. It was created and maintained for the primary purpose of producing goods.
2. It was a large complex "secondary" group.
3. It was part of a still larger organization.
4. It had a pyramidal and hierarchical structure with a single head at the top.

The head of the organization was able to induce others to achieve the purposes for which the organization was established. The leader's and the subordinates' jobs were focused on the achievement of a goal, and this goal was not established as a *personal* requirement of the head. Achieving the goal required an acknowledged *interdependence* between leader and subordinates. The leader not only had to acknowledge this interdependence, but he had to act in a way which showed his dependence on the subordinate group (reciprocal interaction). To achieve results the leader had to *integrate* other needs of subordinates with the requirements of top management. He did this by making technical improvements which not only smoothed out the work flow but which reduced interpersonal conflict as a consequence.

The leader's authority was exercised by his playing a *dual* role. He was the group's representative to higher management, and he was higher management's representative to the plant. Neither role was subordinated to the other, as had been the case under the previous administration. For any given administrative problem the leader's role as agent of higher management was *preceded* by his role as representative of the subordinate group.

The Plant Y experience not only confirmed or modified what McGregor and others have said about the nature of authority. It stimulated some additional ideas which might prove useful in future studies of leadership and authority. These ideas revolve around the kinds of conditions which appear to be present in the effective exercise of authority.

## B. *CONDITIONS OF EFFECTIVE AUTHORITY*

### 1. *"Leeway to Act"*

For a person designated as the head of an organization to be able to induce others to strive toward the over-all goal it is necessary that he be allowed by his superiors a certain degree of "leeway" to exercise his discretion. One can visualize a continuum, one end of which represents complete dictation by higher authorities, the other end representing complete autonomy of action. The point at which the head of an organization can induce others to achieve optimum performance lies somewhere along this continuum. This study does not say where this point is, but it is apparent that one manager's authority was ineffective because he had been subject to "close supervision" by his superiors, while the new manager's "point of authority" was considerably farther along the line in the direction of autonomy.

This "condition of leeway" ties in closely with the principles of authority cited earlier. Only when the leader is granted leeway of action by his superiors can he (*a*) set realistic goals or targets which both he and his subordinates can meet through collaborative effort, (*b*) openly acknowledge interdependence, and (*c*) integrate the productive requirements of the total organization with the immediate needs of subordinates. Permission to act without constant dictation by superiors also makes it possible for the leader to play the dual role both as agent *of* higher authorities and as representative of his organization *to* higher authorities. The substance of the actions he takes in each role may be economic or technical, but the manner in which he keeps one role from dominating the other is essentially a political function.

### 2. *Time Perspective*

In comparing the two managers it has been observed repeatedly that the first manager acted chiefly in response to immediate emergencies while the second manager devoted a greater part of his time to matters related to future planning. From this observation one may hypothesize that a leader's efforts to induce others to meet the organization's productive goals will be successful to the extent that his activities are focused on a longer time perspective. This same hypothesis would appear to hold true for other members at different levels of the organization.[20]

### 3. Horizontal Work-Flow Interaction

The former manager's authority had been less effective because of his exclusive reliance on the formal vertical structure of the organization. In general, information had flowed vertically through the chain of command within one of the formally designated functions (production, inspection, accounting, etc.). After decisions had been made at high levels, the information or directives would then be passed down through the separate channels of the other departments. Each group had been regarded as a distinctly separate function much the way it would appear on the formal organizational chart. Yet technologically the organization was based upon a continuous-flow principle which made it necessary for information to flow along a horizontal plane. Any actual or potential interruption in the work flow often required simultaneous action on the part of members of several structurally "separate" groups.

By not insisting that information on a work-flow problem be transmitted up through the "proper" *and* separate channels for decision and back down through other formal channels, the new manager in effect modified the traditional structure of organization to meet more realistically the technological requirements.

---

[20] Further support for this hypothesis was gained in direct observations of each of 56 assembly line foremen for a full eight-hour day. In an analysis of more than 32,000 incidents it was found that the foremen who had to cope with fewer "emergencies" (*a*) had more time for planning, and (*b*) were judged by others to be more successful. See R. H. Guest, "Of Time and the Foremen," *Personnel*, Vol. 32, No. 6 (May, 1956). Also F. J. Jasinski and R. H. Guest, "Redesigning the Supervisor's Job," *Factory Management and Maintenance*, Vol. 115, No. 12 (December, 1957).

This shift from reliance on a purely vertical structure to recognition of the importance of a horizontal structure has implications for understanding one aspect of authority. It suggests that in a complex hierarchical organization in order for a leader to induce others to work toward a common goal he cannot rely on the vertical system alone. For him to gain the co-operation of subordinates he must also be aware and make use of the horizontal system of communications required by the work flow. This observation, perhaps, may be worth special consideration in the light of the popular preoccupation with the principle of "participative management." Indeed, the present study, using the reciprocal interaction concept, supports much of what has been said about the importance of participation in facilitating healthy vertical relationships. But the study introduces another dimension often overlooked in participative management discussions: The "genius" of Cooley was not simply the use he made of vertical channels. Unlike his predecessor he understood that the system would never function harmoniously if he concentrated on vertical controls and interactions. The required activities of his factory were dominated by technical and work-flow imperatives. He was effective in large measure because he reorganized the interactions along the lines of actual work-flow requirements.

### 4. *Enlarging the Span of Cognition of the Leader and Subordinates*

In an earlier chapter describing phases in the change process, the term "span of cognition" was used. It was observed that supervisors were able to perform their specialized tasks more effectively because they understood better how their particular specialty "fitted into" the whole system of socio-technical relationships. It was also observed that the new manager had developed idea-collecting mechanisms which gave *him* a better understanding of the way the whole organization "fitted together."

This enlargement in the span of cognition by subordinates *and* by the manager is relevant here. Acceptance of the former manager's directives met with considerable resistance inasmuch as these directives were based on limited or fragmented information which he received. It is true that as head of the communications pyramid he was in the best position to see the whole picture. However, by his emphasis on strict separation of departmental functions, his insistence that information flow up the line through the formal vertical channels, and his encouragement of interdepartmental rivalry, the information which he used to issue directives came to him as aggregates of "facts," often unrelated and frequently contradictory. There was little exchange of information among the members *before* it reached the manager.

Under the new manager much information was exchanged between departments and levels preceding its submission to the manager. Facts relevant to one's immediate section were tempered by information which the subordinate received elsewhere. When the manager issued directives on the basis of information he received in this integrated or "predigested" form, subordinates more readily accepted the decisions. And, as has been pointed out earlier, many of the decisions never had to come as high as the manager because those at lower levels had adequate information on which to act themselves.[21]

A conclusion one reaches is that for a leader to induce others to act requires that he establish for himself and for others mechanisms that allow both to be continually enlarging their span of cognition; this enlargement is not merely a greater accumulation of isolated facts and ideas but of facts and ideas that have had broad circulation before they are acted upon.

### 5. *Group Interaction*

In a rationally structured complex organization based on principles of specialization of function, chain of command, and unity of direction, there is no need, theoretically at least,

---

[21] This observation supports that of one of the most successful business administrators, the late Chester I. Barnard, who, according to Eliot Chapple, said, "I only had to make about one *real* decision a year. My organization made the rest for me."

for administrative functions to be carried out through the use of primary groups. The "classical" theorists ignored the primary group and stressed the logical necessity of maintaining an organization through the one-to-one superior/subordinate relationship.

Plant Y's organizational chart and formal position descriptions in both time periods ignored "groups" as a source of administrative action. Even though persons were sometimes referred to as a group, that is, as production or inspection, they could hardly be considered as primary groups as generally defined by the sociologist. Nor could persons holding similar positions, such as foremen, be considered a closely knit, face-to-face group. Their only common denominator was that they happened to occupy a *level* in the organization; in their day-to-day activities they were separated spatially and functionally.

Although it cannot be said that Plant Y under the new manager changed the fundamental one-to-one superior/subordinate administrative system, many decisions were made as a result of meetings of small face-to-face groups. The purpose and effects of such meetings have been analyzed earlier. Viewing them in relation to other conditions of effective authority it can be seen that group meetings (*a*) were instrumental in gaining a "time perspective" for decisions since they were not focused on emergencies, (*b*) they increased the amount of "horizontal work-flow interaction" necessary to this type of technology, and (*c*) they served to enlarge the span of cognition among those participating.

An unanticipated consequence of group participation was that each member gained a feeling of reinforcement and support not provided for in the formal one-to-one system of relationships. Those at higher levels were able to return to their separate sections or departments knowing that they had the support of their peers and superiors. This reinforcement process carried down through each level. There was a reverse process as well. Subordinates having also interacted frequently in a group situation felt they had more "organized" support in bringing suggestions or complaints to those at higher levels. The reinforcement effect was especially important to the manager himself in his dealings with higher officials. It might be added parenthetically that lack of identification with a group from which he could draw support not only reduced the former manager's authority over subordinates but reduced his influence on his superiors. The psychological effect on the former manager was to increase his own feelings of "anomie" which in turn made it even more difficult for him to alter the course of events leading to his removal.

In concluding our observations on group interaction as a condition of effective authority the following summary comment is offered:

Authority cannot be successfully exercised when those in command positions rely solely on the one-to-one superior-subordinate relationship. Many administrative decisions must be generated within and evolve from interactions which take place in primary groups even though such "groups" are rarely provided for in the formal structure of organization. When these groups function effectively they become something more than an additional mechanism of efficient communication. They serve a support and reinforcement function for the individual vis-à-vis subordinates and superiors. At an even deeper level, identification with a primary group serves to counteract the feelings of alienation and "anomie" so characteristic of life in large bureaucratic organizations.

# CHAPTER 9

# Production Organizations as Socio-Technical Systems

Throughout the descriptive and analytical sections of this study frequent use was made of the term "socio-technical system." At the risk of repetition it is appropriate here in the concluding section to expand on the meaning of the term and to point out how the socio-technical system concept might be useful for students of organization theory and for managers of complex enterprises.

The importance of combining the *social* and the *technical* into a unified systems concept was stressed in the introduction:

> On his part the social scientist often makes the error of concentrating on human motivation and group behavior without fully accounting for the technical environment which circumscribes, even determines, the roles which the actors play. Motivation, group structure, interaction processes, authority—none of these abstractions of behavior takes place in a technological vacuum.

In the period of disintegration at Plant Y, it was observed repeatedly that the stress and hostility found in the human relationships were often linked directly to malfunctions in the technical operations of the assembly line. The flow of physical material or the flow of technical information necessary to sustain a smooth input, throughput, and output was subject to frequent interruption or blockage. Each interruption triggered some kind of action. Action was manifested in tension-charged interactions of subordinates, peers, and superiors with back effects throughout the complex hierarchy. Rarely were these interactions concerned solely with an exchange of technical "facts": more often than not what was really being "exchanged" were intense feelings of suspicion, fear, or hostility. The fixing of blame on technical problems became blurred with the fixing of blame on people. Those at higher levels resorted increasingly to bureaucratic weapons of power including the threat of discharge. Subordinates, fearing personal reprisal, found it more difficult to act rationally in the solution of technical problems. The spiraling effect of technical to social to technical continued to the point where the output of their combined efforts no longer met the minimum standards of performance set by a larger component of the system, the parent organization.

The first step taken to keep the ship from foundering was a social act: a new manager was put at the helm. The subsequent acts of the new manager set a new pattern of interpersonal relations, of feelings and perceptions. Subsequent acts of the manager and those below him resulted in technical changes as well. Both aspects of change, the social and technical, combined to generate the upward cycle of improved performance.

The major initial event of change in complex organizations does not have to be a social act, such as the succession of a new top man. It can be technical in the sense, for example, that plant layout can be entirely revamped and new machines installed with no changes in the personnel who direct the operations. It is only stating the obvious to say that the moment changes in the technical system are begun, the relationships between members of the human organization also begin to change. The degree of success or lack of success depends on management's skills in anticipating the reciprocal effect of technology and organization.

It is this reciprocity of men and technology which leads one to conclude that a basic unit of organization in our society, the factory, is best described not as a social system alone nor as a technical system but as a socio-technical system. Trist and Bamforth in England first suggested the term some years ago in their classic study of the conversion to the long-wall method of coal mining.[1] As a result of studies of steel mills, chemical factories, aircraft engine plants, and especially the present study of Plant Y, this observer believes that the socio-technical system concept is both a useful and necessary way of looking at complex production organizations.

Central to this system concept is the input, throughput, output process with each of the three dimensions of the process having continuous influence on the other. The elements sustaining the process are men and technological devices, the former including the social organization and the latter including both physical facilities and rationally conceived mechanisms for sustaining a continuous work flow.

In the present study the system unit being analyzed is the factory, but the concept can be applied to smaller and to larger units. It can apply microcosmically to the study of stress in work groups within an enterprise or to the universal effects of the shift from the "putting-out" system to the factory system in the early period of the Industrial Revolution.

Taking a systems approach either in the solution of practical problems or in setting up a model for analyzing change in organizations is certainly not a new idea. Engineers, production planners, persons involved in operations research, and many others in business enterprises are thoroughly at home with the systems approach. They clearly understand how changes in technology have an effect on the input, throughput, output process. Skilled administrators and those studying human behavior in complex organizations also use a systemic approach showing how changes in interpersonal relations have an effect on the same basic process.

The modest plea being made here is that the technologist and behaviorist need to be brought together more often than they have in the past. Traditionally technical planning usually precedes the planning for optimum utilization of human resources. Both aspects of planning should be shared jointly and

---

[1] E. L. Trist and K. W. Bamforth, "Some Social and Psychological Consequences of the Long Wall Method of Coal-Getting," *Human Relations,* Vol. 4, No. 1 (1951), pp. 3–38.

simultaneously making use of a socio-technical system concept suggested by this study. Such an effort should not be too difficult for those on either side of the fence who have come to realize that a particular problem to be solved in an enterprise is a product of many forces acting and reacting on one another, and that enumerating specific causes and specific consequent effects in the conventional framework of problem analysis is not very rewarding.

It is possible that the products of science itself will give a strong nudge to those who continue to think in terms of the conventional framework of problem analysis. The input, throughput, output processes of automatic computers are based on a systems principle. Those who are to make effective use of computers as substitutes for human organs of decision and effort must themselves first learn to look at organization problems as products of a total system of human and technical relationships.

# Review of Research

In the course of preparing the present study the author collected a considerable amount of bibliographical material on organization, change, and leadership. Some of the concepts were used in the study; others were not. This appendix is the author's attempt to make use of the Bibliography as an orientation to those who might wish to explore these subject areas further. As an orientation it does not pretend to exhaust the subject; it merely highlights some of the work of other researchers. Where appropriate, particular references are linked to the Plant Y study.

This review of the literature revolves around three primary questions:

1. In a rationally structured formal organization what are the forces at work which lead to tension and stress among its members?
2. What is the process over time by which tension and stress may be reduced and performance improved?
3. What is the role of the leader in the change process?

A definition of terms and a statement of assumptions included in these questions are in order. "Organization" as used here tentatively means a large group of persons engaged in mutually dependent activities for a specific purpose. It is a secondary group and can be distinguished from the face-to-face primary group by its size and complexity. "Rationally structured" means:

a) That the organization has been formed as a legal entity at some identifiable point in time and space.

*b*) That men and physical objects have been deliberately brought together to achieve a defined goal.

*c*) That the manner in which the task is to be accomplished is based on calculation and reason, which distinguish it from spontaneous formation or from "traditional" organization.

*d*) That the arrangement of men and material objects assumes a form generally recognized and agreed to by the participants.

"Formal" refers only to the fact that those responsible for maintaining the existence of the organization can describe its form in language and symbols, such as charts and manuals.

"Tension" and "stress" are symbolic expressions of conflict. They are used here to refer not only to internal states in persons but also to the behavior that individuals manifest in their relations with others.

"Process" denotes progressive actions or a series of acts performed by persons in the course of moving the organization from one state to another. Process also implies some regularity of action.

The assumption underlying the questions above is, of course, that tension exists in varying degrees in any social relationship in which one person or group defines a goal for others and directs their activity toward achieving this goal. A further assumption is that no set of social relationships is static; patterns are constantly undergoing change in time.

## A. *SOURCES OF TENSION AND STRESS IN ORGANIZATIONS*

The *raison d'être* of an industrial unit such as a factory is the efficient production of material goods for a profit; the factory's primary and immediate purpose is economic, not social; its operation is based on rational principles.

These principles have been described in various ways. They have been applied to the manipulation of materials in a strict engineering sense and to the direction of men in an organization sense. Mass production, in terms of machines and materials, involves the *standardization* of physical objects so that they are *interchangeable*. The machines must function at optimum speed and with *predictable* precision. Movement in time and space must be synchronized and continuous.[1]

Rational principles when applied to the organization of men (particularly Weber's "pure" bureaucratic type) are not very different from principles applied to the manipulation of materials. As Merton stated it: "The chief merit of bureaucracy is its technical efficiency, with a premium placed on precision, speed, expert control, continuity, discretion, and optimum returns on in-put."[2]

Whether the principles of human organization of industry were derived from the principles of machine operation, or whether historically the reverse was true is of little importance, for they function simultaneously. Both are rational and mechanistic. Merton went on to say: ". . . it becomes plain to all who would see that man is to a very important degree controlled by his social relations to the instruments of production."[3]

Frederick Taylor, father of "scientific management," had a profound effect on industrial organizations. The results of his work affected the design of tasks at the basic work level—the direct man/machine relationship.[4] Efficiency, Taylor held, can be achieved when tasks are broken down into their simplest constituent motions. Taylor looked upon the worker as essentially an extension of the machine itself, but, because workers were subject to error, he held it necessary to specialize man's tasks and make them repetitive. Every effort should be made to eliminate the element of human judgment by the operator. Such judgment should be exercised by experts and should be based upon scientific motion and time studies. Carefully planned controls should be established so that maximum productivity and quality of output are achieved. These controls, based upon rational principles, justified the establishment of what are commonly known today as "service," "control," and "reporting" functions. The emergence and growth of these

---

[1] Roger Burlingame, *Backgrounds of Power*, p. 15.
[2] Robert K. Merton, *Social Theory and Social Structure*, p. 196.
[3] *Ibid.*, p. 197.
[4] Frederick W. Taylor, *Scientific Management*.

groups ancillary to the central "production" function have complicated socio-technical systems measurably.

While Taylor later became concerned with the structure of the factory system at higher managerial levels, it remained for others to explain and to justify the use of rational principles in the organization of management. Among these were men such as Dennison,[5] Fayol,[6] Urwick,[7] and Brown.[8] All agreed that each activity in the organization must of logical necessity be specialized. *Specialization* occurs not only at the work level but throughout all levels as a function of the division of labor. Offices at successively higher levels in the line are vested with progressively greater powers. The process by which the powers are vested at each level involves the *chain of command* principle. There is a "mathematical" limit to which members of different levels can direct and control subordinates. This principle has come to be known as *span of control*.[9] Since the various units of an organization engage in activities that are relatively homogeneous, those in positions of control of units give directions to their own subordinates, not to members of other units. This principle is labeled *unity of direction*.[10]

These same rational principles find expression in much of Weber's postulates about bureaucracy, that form of administrative organization which he said is "from a purely technical point of view, capable of attaining the highest degree of efficiency."[11] Weber spoke of specialization, a hierarchy of authority, and systems of controls based on rationally determined rules and regulations.

Weber went on from his postulates to establish the "ideal type" of formal organization; it included among others the elements mentioned above. Merton's summary of Weber's ideal type states that among the required characteristics are the

[5] Henry S. Dennison, *Organization Engineering*.

[6] Henri Fayol, *General and Industrial Management*.

[7] Lyndall F. Urwick, *The Elements of Administration*.

[8] Alvin Brown, *Organization of Industry*.

[9] Luther Gulick and Lyndall F. Urwick, *Papers on the Science of Administration*.

[10] Chris Argyris, *Personality and Organization*, p. 3.

[11] Max Weber, *The Theory of Social and Economic Organization*, p. 337.

... clear-cut division of integrated activities which are regarded as duties inherent in the regulations. The assignment of roles ... on the basis of technical qualifications ... ascertained through formalized, impersonal procedures. ... Within the structure of hierarchically arranged authority, the activities of "trained and salaried experts" are governed by general, abstract, and clearly defined rules which preclude the necessity for the issuance of specific instructions for each specific case. The ... official is appointed, ... not elected.[12]

Two abstract concepts are included in Weber's discussion of the ideal type of the rational goal-oriented organization. It is essential, Weber held, that the power to direct action be vested not in an individual as such, but in the *office* which the individual occupies. This is the bureaucratic concept called "impersonality." Also, if the organization is to function efficiently, the rules and regulations must be followed in precise and orderly fashion. This is the concept known as "discipline."

These abstractions take on specific meaning only when related, as this study has tried to do, to the continuing behavior of actual persons in an actual socio-technical environment in a time dimension.

What has been said so far can be summarized as follows: The efficient production of material goods in a large-scale organization requires the application of certain rational or logical principles. Men have described these abstract principles as they relate to the organization of machines and materials and as they relate to the organization of human beings. Task specialization, a hierarchy of positions endowed with differing degrees of authority, a rationally ordered system of controls reinforced by a disciplined acceptance of impersonally conceived and administered rules—these are some of the central elements of rational purposive organization.

It is obvious that these principles or concepts have been applied in large measure to industrial organizations since the beginning of the Industrial Revolution; the results in terms of output and efficiency are apparent. However, Merton,[13]

---

[12] Merton, *op. cit.*, p. 195.
[13] *Ibid.*, p. 123.

Argyris,[14] and many others have suggested that the logical application of concepts of "scientific management" or of Weber's bureaucracy can create tension and stress leading to inefficiency, disintegration, and "dysfunction."

There appears to be general agreement that the requirements of formal organization and the needs of individuals and groups within the organization are not always congruent. Malinowski, for example, using his familiar concept of "institution," held that every institution should not only contribute "toward the integral working of the community as a whole," but should satisfy "the desires and basic needs of the individual as well."[15]

Ellsworth refined Malinowski's concepts of institutional functions in the more specific context of industry. In his study of the New Freedom Products Company he found it useful to separate those functions of an institution "which satisfy directly the needs of the personnel" from those "which meet the organizational or operational needs of the institution."[16] Ellsworth called the former "consummatory functions" and the latter "instrumental functions" or "organizational requirements." Ellsworth then showed how in his industrial plant's history the organizational requirements established by the owners and managers were often in conflict with the needs of members of the organization in subordinate positions.

Jacobson, Charters, and Lieberman, approaching the study of organization by using the "role concept," observed that behavior expectations can differ markedly depending upon one's position or status in the organization. Where there is at any given time a "degree of consensus or sharing of expectations about the behavior of people who occupy various positions," then, these observers held, "a degree of integration existed within the organization."[17] Granted that the abstract

[14] Argyris, op. cit., p. 13.

[15] Bronislaw Malinowski, A Scientific Theory of Culture, p. 52.

[16] John S. Ellsworth, Factory Folkways, p. 101.

[17] Eugene Jacobson, W. W. Charters, Jr., and Seymour Lieberman, "The Use of the Role Concept in the Study of Complex Organization," Journal of Social Issues, Vol. 7, No. 3 (1951), p. 20.

term "integration" requires a clearer operational definition, there is implicit in these findings a separation between what Ellsworth, Bakke,[18] and Argyris call the "formal organizational requirements" expressed by those in higher positions of the hierarchy and what they call the "individual or group needs" felt by those at lower levels. As the present study of Plant Y demonstrated, *the difference between the two determines the degree of tension and stress likely to be found in the organization.*

Sargent spoke of differing roles in the hierarchical organization, stressing that "the smooth functioning of group activities requires a hierarchical organization and more or less stabilized roles." Stability can be achieved only when those in different positions hold "reciprocal expectations" toward one another.[19] Sargent's postulate can be illustrated by a situation from industrial experience: A group of foremen do not expect that their general foreman should issue direct orders to hourly workers. When the general foreman accepts this norm and consistently allows his foremen to issue the orders, then their mutual role expectations are reciprocal.

Kahn and Morse, although they take a different approach and use different referents to explain their data on productivity and morale, arrive at conclusions consistent with those of other observers. As they put it: "One criterion of organizational effectiveness then becomes the extent to which the organization facilitates or thwarts the maximization of need satisfaction on the part of the members."[20]

This is precisely the theme upon which Argyris has developed the thesis that the needs of an organization are often in basic conflict with the needs of its members. Argyris said:

> It is concluded that the formal organization principles make demands of relatively healthy individuals that are incongruent with their needs. Frustration, conflict, failure, and short time perspec-

[18] E. Wight Bakke, *Adaptive Human Behavior.*

[19] S. Stansfield Sargent, "Conceptions of Role and Ego in Contemporary Psychology," in John H. Rohrer and Muzafer Sherif (eds.), *Social Psychology at the Crossroads,* p. 395.

[20] Robert L. Kahn and Nancy C. Morse, "The Relationship of Productivity to Morale," *Journal of Social Issues,* Vol. 7, No. 3 (1951), p. 8.

tive are predicted as resultants of this basic incongruency. . . .
The basic impact of the formal organization structure is to make
employees feel dependent, submissive, and passive, and to require
them to utilize only a few of their less important abilities.[21]

Katz singles out some of the principles of formal organization already described earlier (centralization in the command
chain and limited span of control) and states that the principles "take no account of the possibilities of group responsibility and the resulting motivation."[22]

Suojanen raises further questions about traditional assumptions of the effectiveness of formal hierarchical organizations
and about the principles of impersonality and routinization:
"In spite of popular beliefs, even the military has begun to
recognize that hierarchy alone is a woefully inadequate means
for developing identification on the part of the individual toward the organization. Basic to the original philosophy of
military hierarchy is the concept of command as the technique
of administration."[23]

After pointing out that the military hierarchy is essentially
a bureaucracy, as are other complex organizations with a "rational orientation toward particular goals and objectives,"
Suojanen comments on the characteristics of impersonality
and routinization referred to earlier.

> Impersonality implies that the job and the employee are com-
> pletely separated so that communication occurs between offices
> rather than between people. Furthermore, routinization means
> that activities are simple and regular so that the results can be
> judged solely by the criterion of efficiency.
>
> Economic theory, military hierarchy, bureaucracy, and formal
> organization theory . . . ignore almost wholly the informal or-
> ganization that operates within the formal, and they pay scant
> attention to the values which are held by the . . . participants
> within the system.[24]

---

[21] Argyris, op. cit., p. 74.

[22] Daniel Katz, Introduction to "Human Relations Research in Large Organizations,"
Journal of Social Issues, Vol. 7, No. 3 (1951), p. 4.

[23] Waino W. Suojanen, "Leadership, Authority and the Span of Control," Advanced
Management, Vol. 22, No. 9 (September, 1957), p. 18.

[24] Ibid., p. 10.

The observations of Merton, Blau, and Gouldner are especially relevant here. In his discussion of "deviant" behavior,
Merton begins by properly dismissing the notion that such
behavior is "the accidental result of . . . pathological personalities found in these groups and strata."[25] Merton insists that
there are often built-in discrepancies between the requirements of a secondary group, such as one structured according
to bureaucratic principles, and the social requirements of persons working from day to day in primary groups. The contra-
dictions can create what Merton calls "dysfunctions."[26] When
these occur in a given social system, whether it be a factory or
any other large purposive group, the system fails to fulfill its
chosen objectives. In time either the organization ceases to
exist, or the tensions "may be instrumental in leading to
changes in the system."[27]

Conformity to regulations is a central requirement of bureaucracy. This requirement, Merton explains, "can be dys-
functional both for realizing the objectives of the structure
and for the various groups in the society which the bureaucracy is intended to serve." Rules, regulations, and orders, all
designed as means for improving efficiency, can lead to inefficiency when the members of an organization come to feel
that "following the rules" is more immediately rewarding
than "getting the job done efficiently." Merton puts it this
way: "Adherence to rules originally conceived as a means becomes transformed into an end in itself. . . . This emphasis,
resulting from the displacement of the original goals, develops
into rigidities and an inability to adjust readily."[28]

Blau carries this reasoning further. If members of an organization are supposed to exercise impersonal detachment in
conforming to rationally conceived regulations and orders,
"it is unlikely that high *esprit de corps* will develop among [the
members]. The strict exercise of authority in the interest of
discipline induces subordinates, anxious to be highly thought

[25] Merton, *op. cit.*, p. 121.
[26] *Ibid.*, p. 123.
[27] *Ibid.*
[28] *Ibid.*

of by their superiors, to conceal defects in operations from superiors, and this obstruction of the flow of information upward in the hierarchy impedes affective management." [29]

Blau points out certain inconsistencies in Weber's ideal type of rational organization. "No system of rules and regulations can be so finely spun that it anticipates all exigencies that may arise. Changes in external conditions create new administrative problems, and the very innovations introduced to solve them often have unanticipated consequences that produce further problems." [30]

Finally, Blau suggests, emphasis on rule enforcement ignores the fact that men, when placed together in a work relationship, develop their own "rules" (or norms) of behavior. These unofficial standards may either hinder achievement *or* enhance the possibility of achieving efficient operations. Refusal of management to recognize such informal practices tends to lead only to a further proliferation of rules and to further strain. [31]

Gouldner, drawing upon his empirical observations in a gypsum plant, reinforces many of the conclusions above. He says that:

> . . . rules proliferate when a social organization is riven by the following tensions: (*a*) managerial distrust and suspicion become pervasive and are directed not only toward workers, but also toward members of the managerial ingroup as well. (*b*) Disturbances in the informal system which result in the withholding of consent from the formally constituted authorities: the informal group is either unwilling or unable to allocate work responsibilities and gives no support to management's production expectations. (*c*) The appearance of status distinctions of dubious legitimacy, in an egalitarian culture context, which strain the formal authority relationships. [32]

One quickly recognizes how well these observations fit the description of Plant Y in Time Period I.

A review of what others have said about rational organiza-

[29] Peter M. Blau, *Bureaucracy in Modern Society*, p. 33.

[30] *Ibid.*, p. 58.

[31] *Ibid.*, p. 59.

[32] Alvin W. Gouldner, *Patterns of Industrial Bureaucracy*, p. 180.

tion and its impact on individuals and groups would not be complete without some recognition of the fact that strain and tension are related to expectations that people hold and that are conditioned by the culture beyond the factory gates. The factory is not a closed system, even though this study appears to treat it as such. From childhood onward people play a number of roles in nonworking hours which are often quite different from those demanded of them when they enter the office or shop.

Znaniecki, for example, was not referring to the immediate factory situation as such in one of his cogent observations, but he did stress the need to understand the broader "universal" patterns in the culture as they condition the immediate situation.[33]

Superior-to-subordinate behavior in an industrial setting, Gouldner found, was considered legitimate when superiors employed criteria "applicable to the relations among friends and neighbors, rather than in a *business* and *industrial* context."[34]

Arensberg cited examples in the community-factory context to show that behavior in the plant situation was often largely conditioned by established culture patterns outside the factory.[35]

Roethlisberger and Dickson spell out some of the norms of behavior, particularly in the father-son relationship, which develop in a community but are not necessarily logical or "efficient." They conclude: "The criterion in terms of which the supervisor [in a factory] must exercise discipline is not the convention of ordinary social living but a logic of efficiency. . . . It is this insistence upon a logic of efficiency, this continued attempt to force the human organization into logical molds that creates constraint."[36]

---

[33] Florian Znaniecki, *The Social Role of the Man of Knowledge.*

[34] Gouldner, *op. cit.,* p. 55.

[35] Conrad M. Arensberg, "Industry and Community," *American Journal of Sociology,* Vol. 27, No. 4 (July, 1942).

[36] Fritz Roethlisberger and William Dickson, *Management and the Worker,* p. 457.

In a similar manner, Jacques, in his study of the changing culture of the factory, concludes: ". . . patterns of behavior and organization within the concern must remain consistent with the patterns of behavior and expectations of a community that carries this culture."[37]

From the approach of personality development, Argyris lists seven assumptions as to how the personality of the child develops into that of the mature adult. Among these seven are the following:

> That the child develops from a state of dependence to a state of relative independence as an adult.

> That human beings as infants are limited in their behavior to a short time perspective. When they become adults, their behavior is influenced by a longer time perspective, both past and future.

> That children hold a distinctly subordinate position, but as adults they aspire "to occupy an equal and/or superordinate position relative to their peers.[38]

Argyris then spells out his central thesis—namely, that the imperatives of the formal organizational structure of the plant tend to ignore or deny these facts of personality growth which have their origins in the outside culture.

## B. THE PROCESS BY WHICH STRAIN AND TENSION CAN BE MODIFIED

"All science or disinterested itellectual inquiry ultimately seeks knowledge of process."[39] The term "process," denoting progressive actions or series of acts or steps in a regular course of moving from one state to another, is reasonably well understood in physical science and mechanics. In the social sciences, and especially in the study of behavior changes in large complex groups, not much is known about the processes that generate change.

There have been, of course, many studies describing ob-

---

[37] Eliot Jacques, *The Changing Culture of a Factory*, p. 260.

[38] Chris Argyris, "Organizational Leadership and Participative Management," *Journal of Business of the University of Chicago*, Vol. 28, No. 1 (January, 1955), p. 4.

[39] A. L. Kroeber, "Critical Summary and Commentary," in Robert F. Spencer (ed.), *Method and Perspective in Anthropology*, pp. 273-74.

served changes in social structure at different intervals of time, including those of Whyte,[40] Walker,[41] Jacques,[42] Ellsworth,[43] Rice,[44] Dalton,[45] Mann,[46] Ginsberg and Reilly,[47] to name a few in the industrial sphere. Lippitt, Watson, and Wesley advanced certain postulates about "planned" change.[48] Bakke has constructed an elaborate conceptual scheme for describing the "fusion process" by which individual needs and organization requirements are brought into "equilibrium." [49]

These studies have contributed to a better understanding of how patterns of behavior can be modified. Certainly they are more helpful than the descriptions of static properties of organization which one finds either in Weber or among the latter-day exponents of efficient management organization. As Gouldner observes, speaking of Weber's concept of bureacratic authority, "He never systematically analyzed the actual social processes which either generated or thwarted the emergence of consent." [50]

Perhaps the most important effect of these studies of industrial change is the rejection of the notion that change can somehow be explained by enumerating and weighing many "factors" that cause a social system to move from one state to another. What has emerged from past studies is less emphasis on any one factor (e.g., "good" supervision, "proper" span of control, fewer hierarchical levels) and a growing emphasis on what Arensberg and Tootell call the "unfolding process with laws of growth of its own in which factors appear not only in

---

[40] William F. Whyte, *Pattern for Industrial Peace.*

[41] Charles R. Walker, *Toward the Automatic Factory.*

[42] Jacques, *op. cit.*

[43] Ellsworth, *op. cit.*

[44] A. K. Rice, "The Experimental Reorganization of Non-Automatic Weaving in an Indian Mill," *Human Relations,* Vol. 8, No. 3 (August, 1955).

[45] Melville Dalton, "Conflicts between Staff and Line Managerial Officers," *American Sociological Review,* Vol. 15, No. 3 (June, 1950).

[46] Floyd C. Mann, "Changing Superior-Subordinate Relationships," *Journal of Social Issues,* Vol. 7, No. 3 (1951).

[47] Eli Ginsberg and Ewing W. Reilly, *Effecting Change in Large Organizations.*

[48] Ronald Lippitt, Jeanne Watson, and Bruce Wesley, *The Dynamics of Planned Change.*

[49] E. Wight Bakke, *Organization and the Individual.*

[50] Gouldner, *op. cit.,* p. 223.

great or small degree but also in a *necessary order of occurrence.*[51]

Leighton speaks of any given item of behavior as "a product of multiple, interacting forces, rather than the result of a single cause that can be ferreted out like a detective uncovering a murderer."[52]

Sherif warns the social psychologists against the factorial approach to social process by saying: "The task is to go beyond the general statement that everything is related to everything else within the frame of reference and laboriously to vary this factor now, that factor later, with the ultimate aim of finding the relative weights for each and, finally, expressing the relations in short-cut expressions."[53]

Homans, after stressing the simultaneous interdependence of interaction, sentiment, and activity, goes on to observe that: "Social change may start in any part of the system, through changes in the external system of the group, alterations in its physical environment, technical organization, or even its internal system, and will, of course, have back effects of a greater or lesser order on all of these."[54]

Merton establishes useful guide lines for analyzing change in complex organizations. His suggestion that stresses inherent in bureacratic structures can lead to dysfunction and ultimate change is key to the central question of how tension and stress may be modified.[55]

The principle of "group reinforcement" has been suggested as an approach to understanding how social stress can be modified and changed. Newcomb observes that: "The more *frequently* and the more obviously group members demonstrate by their behavior that a certain kind of role is prescribed by the group norms, the more vividly they call to one another's

---

[51] Conrad M. Arensberg and Geoffrey Tootell, "Plant Sociology," in Mirra Komarovsky (ed.), *Common Frontiers of the Social Sciences*, p. 316.

[52] Alexander H. Leighton, *Human Relations in a Changing World*, p. 159.

[53] Muzafer Sherif, "Introduction," in John H. Rohrer and Muzafer Sherif (eds.), *Social Psychology at the Crossroads*, pp. 4-5.

[54] Henry W. Rieken and George C. Homans, "Psychological Aspects of Social Structure," in Gardner Lindzey (ed.), *Handbook of Social Psychology*, Vol. II, p. 825.

[55] Merton, *op. cit.*, p. 123.

attention what the role prescriptions are, and the more they intensify one another's motivation to take their own 'proper' role." [56]

Newcomb does not say precisely how this process takes place, but his suggestion of a *frequency* rate which changes over time seems to move us a little closer to a less abstract notion of what process is. In the present study considerable use was made of the descriptive term "interaction frequencies" as a basic term for describing behavior.

Some have suggested that *greater participation in the decision-making process* will lead to a reduction in organizational stress. Coch and French demonstrated this by showing that productivity of an industrial work group increased when members of the organization were permitted to participate as a group in designing techniques for coping with changes in manufacturing methods. [57]

Leavitt observed that in a complex organization the greatest productivity was achieved when there was a "high degree of participation, maximum joint responsibility for decision-making, and maximum freedom of expression." [58] He went on to point out that the authoritarian hierarchical design of most organizations makes participation difficult but that "an effective compromise is possible." [59] But Leavitt, as with so many others, does not fully spell out what happens to the group internally and to its performance over time after it has been allowed to participate in decisions. Arensberg's suggestion that it would be "useful to study changes in productivity and morale periodically after participation had been introduced," [60] is one which gave encouragement to the Plant Y study.

---

[56] Theodore M. Newcomb, "Social Psychological Theory: Integrating Individual and Social Approaches," in John H. Rohrer and Muzafer Sherif (eds.), *Social Psychology at the Crossroads,* p. 44.

[57] Lester Coch and John R. P. French, Jr., "Overcoming Resistance to Change," *Human Relations,* Vol. 1, No. 4, (1948).

[58] Harold Leavitt, "Small Groups in Large Organizations," *Journal of Business of the University of Chicago,* Vol. 28, No. 1 (January, 1955), p. 12.

[59] *Ibid.,* p. 17.

[60] Conrad M. Arensberg, "Behavior and Organization," p. 338.

The truth seems to be that we still know too little about the way in which organizational stress is modified. The simple question has not been asked enough: "Who does what, when, where, how, with whom, and how often?" As Arensberg put it: "What remains to be discovered about the process of group facilitation of achievement is, unfortunately, still nearly everything." [61]

Time, of course, is the crucial dimension. It follows logically that the data for studying change should be collected not at a single unit of time but either continuously or at intervals. "Only by comparing different structures in a time series can one discover whether a system has manifested self-maintaining processes or processes of change, short-term or long-term." [62]

Measurement of complex socio-psychological processes in a series of time intervals has been one of Lazarsfeld's primary concerns for many years in his studies of voting habits. His observations on studies of folk society are relevant to studies of industrial organizations. As he put it: "To the best of our knowledge there is too little 'timed' material available to carry out such an inquiry into changes of the folk society." [63]

Viewing what others have said about the process of change, there is a pattern of agreement as to the source of tension and stress and as to the necessary conditions for their reduction. Controls imposed by persons at the top of the hierarchy do not assure either efficiency or the co-operation of subordinates. There must be some kind of involvement from below which makes it possible for subordinates to accept changes and even to initiate a certain amount of change themselves. Put in the form of a general hypothesis: in a complex organization tension and stress will diminish and performance will improve with the introduction of social mechanisms which permit those in subordinate positions to participate in making de-

---

[61] Arensberg and Tootell, op. cit., p. 318.

[62] Bernard Barber, "Structural-Functional Analysis: Some Problems and Misunderstandings," American Sociological Review, Vol. 21, No. 2 (April, 1956), p. 133.

[63] Paul F. Lazarsfeld, "Problems in Methodology," in Robert K. Merton, Leonard Broom, and Leonard S. Cottrell, Jr. (eds.), Sociology Today—Problems and Prospects, p. 75.

cisions affecting their present and future roles in the organization.

It was one of the purposes of this study to test this hypothesis in a live organization subjected to change over time. Specifically, the author wished to explore what the overworked term "participation" really means as an action process.

## C. *THE ROLE OF THE LEADER IN THE PROCESS OF CHANGE*

Organizations undergo change as a result of a number of internal and external forces acting upon them. New technology may be introduced. New markets are found and new products are developed. Scientific and engineering innovations can have marked effects in stimulating change as can external economic conditions.

But specific actions to initiate change are taken by *people* and, complex organizations being what they are, those at the head are the primary change agents. More needs to be known about the actions by persons in positions of leadership that start the change process going. This study focused on the plant manager as the primary initiator of change.

Most of the early studies of leadership were concerned with enumerating inherent "traits" of personality which somehow could be associated with successful leadership. It was found, for example, that a successful leader "must have intelligence and good judgment, insight and imagination, ability to accept responsibility, a sense of humor, a well-balanced personality, and a sense of justice." [64]

Such traits, if one could accept some sort of vague operational meaning for these abstractions, were, indeed, found in some successful men. But in time more people studying more leaders added more traits, and in the end no one could find a leader who "possessed" at any given time most or all of these traits. Cromwell, Ghandi, Carrie Nation, Father Divine, and Andrew Carnegie seemed to have little in common as far as personality was concerned.

---

[64] J. A. C. Brown, *The Social Psychology of Industry*, p. 219.

The continued attempt to seek out personality traits of leaders was not entirely useless. Stogdill, in his review of some of the more sophisticated research, was able to show that under certain circumstances such factors as those loosely labeled "intelligence," "initiative," "persistence," "ambition," "dominance," and "surgency" (extroversion), could be found among most persons who influenced the behavior of others.[65] It cannot be denied that the continued refinement of personality tests has been of pragmatic value in the selection of supervisors and managers. But as Sanford reminds us, "the search for 'leadership traits' . . . has not been very rewarding."[66]

The search for traits led to the study of the kinds of observed behavior that effective leaders display. Emphasis on the characteristics of *behavior* was the point of departure for the long and detailed investigation of Hemphill and his colleagues in the Ohio State University Studies. They started by defining leadership as "behavior of an individual when he is directing the activities of a group toward a shared goal."[67] They set up nine a priori dimensions of leadership behavior; after a series of observations they reduced the number to four. These dimensions, or characteristics of behavior, were labeled:

*Consideration*—the concern of a leader for others in carrying out his functions.

*Initiating Structure*—the clarity with which the leader defines the relationship between himself and his subordinates or peers.

*Production Emphasis*—those examples of behavior by which the leader stresses getting the job done.

*Sensitivity or Social Awareness*—acceptance in relation to others.

Subsequent efforts of Fleishman and his colleagues have been

---

[65] Ralph M. Stogdill, "Personal Factors Associated with Leadership: A Survey of the Literature," *Journal of Psychology*, Vol. 25 (1948), pp. 35–71.

[66] Fillmore H. Sanford, "The Follower's Role in Leadership Phenomena," in Guy E. Swanson, Theodore M. Newcomb, and Eugene L. Hartley (eds.), *Readings in Social Psychology*, p. 328.

[67] A. W. Halpin and B. J. Winer, *The Leadership Behavior of the Airplane Commander*, p. 6.

to test the relative importance of these behavioral characteristics.[68]

Other labels have also been applied to leadership behavior:
Lippitt and White's "authoritarian, democratic, or laissez-
faire" types;[69] Haythorn and Couch's "equalitarian" or
"authoritarian" leaders.[70] Others used similar descriptive symbols to score leaders along a dominance-submission continuum.

One criticism of enumerating behavior characteristics and
relating them to group performance has been, as Arensberg
and Tootell point out, that this kind of analytical procedure
does not tell what leaders' actions in a time sequence bring out
what responses. Those who enumerate behavior characteristics
fail to "bring their psychological terms down to operational
definition in the concrete."[71]

From a sociological point of view the enumeration of behavior characteristics of leaders has serious limitations because
it neglects or does not place adequate emphasis on the social and
technical system of which the leader is a part. Acceptance of a
leader in the primary group, for instance, comes *from* the
group and should be regarded as a "patterned social relationship" involving both leader *and* followers.[72] The fact that a
leader possesses the qualities of "consideration" or of "sensitivity" or of being "democratic" or "authoritarian" does not
explain why or how a person obtains and maintains his
authority to induce others to act.

Homans observed that "to rank high in his group, a man
must live up to all of its norms, and the norms . . . must be the
actual or sanctioned norms and not just those to which the
group gives lip service."[73] To bring about action in others involves the concept of authority, which Homans, influenced

[68] Edwin A. Fleishman has reduced the number to two: consideration and initiating
structure. (Personal conversation with the author, October, 1958.)

[69] Ronald Lippitt and R. K. White, "The Social Climate of Children's Groups," in R. G.
Barker, J. S. Kounin, and H. F. Whyte (eds.), *Child Behavior and Development.*

[70] William Haythorn, A. S. Couch, *et al.* "The Behavior of Authoritarian and Equalitarian Personalities in Groups," *Human Relations,* Vol. 9, No. 1 (February, 1956).

[71] Arensberg and Tootell, *op. cit.,* p. 326.

[72] Merton, *op. cit.,* p. 339.

[73] George C. Homans, *The Human Group,* p. 141.

by Barnard, defined this way: "If an order given by a leader to a member of his group is accepted by the member and controls his activity in the group, then the order is said to have authority." [74] Suojanen calls authority the "*right* to make decisions which are accepted by others as a basis for action." [75] Merton, on the subject of authority and norms, says, "Orders will ordinarily not be accepted if they depart considerably from the norms operating within the group." [76] Pelz sets forth a similar postulate by stating that "the more the leader . . . helps other members achieve their goals, the greater will be the members' acceptance of him." [77]

Gibb, in summarizing his interactional theory of leadership (Note: "interaction" in Gibb's terms is not to be confused with the limited meaning of interaction used in this study) points out that effective leadership "is relative to the group task and goal . . . the goal determines the needs which he [the leader] must appear to satisfy . . . ." [78]

These definitions and postulates are generally accepted today by the sociologist and social psychologist. One of the tasks of this study was to find out how two leaders of the same group in different time periods acted in such a way as to satisfy or not to satisfy the needs of the subordinate organization, while at the same time they both tried to carry out a clear-cut mandate to show results.

The concept of the leader's behaving in accordance with the needs and expectations of subordinates is a useful point of departure, but it is also much too simple. One envies those who deal solely with the leader's behavior in the group under experimental conditions or where the "real-life" group is relatively small and uncontaminated by many external forces. The researcher's problem and, indeed, the leader's own problems

---

[74] *Ibid.*, p. 418.

[75] Suojanen, *op. cit.*, p. 19.

[76] Merton, *op. cit.*, p. 340.

[77] Donald C. Pelz, "Leadership within a Hierarchical Organization," *Journal of Social Issues*, Vol. 7, No. 3 (1951), p. 49.

[78] Cecil A. Gibb, "Leadership," in Gardner Lindzey (ed.), *Handbook of Social Psychology*, Vol. II, p. 915.

become vastly more complicated when the social "group" is a large multilevel organization of more than 4,000 persons and is but one of 126 units of a still larger organization staffed by more than a half million employees. The leader of one unit under these circumstances is a "follower" as well as a leader. How the leader acts effectively in this dual role was a major challenge of this study.

McGregor, whose observations were cited extensively in the analytical sections of this study, clearly saw the importance of examining the leader's dual role.[79] McGregor recognized the conflicts which often arise in carrying out this dual role, but he held that the conflicts can be minimized:

a) When the leader wholly acknowledges his dependence upon subordinates.

b) When the leader and subordinates "set targets" which are worked out in a collaborative effort.

c) When subordinates perceive that their own needs will be best fulfilled when they work toward the goals of the organization.

Writers in the Weber tradition have pointed out that when heads of organizations utilize only their formal powers, they are unable to find out about the needs of subordinates and act in accordance with them. The manager in Gouldner's study, upon succeeding to office, found that he had to rely increasingly upon "punishment-centered" actions to force production results.[80] No matter how much he demonstrated to his superiors how well he was carrying out *their* orders, the group below resisted, and resistance was strongest in the one area of the organization which over the years had developed uniform and strong reinforcing norms concerning what its members considered to be "legitimate" actions on management's part.

Gouldner's punishment-centered mode of leadership is called "directive" by Argyris, who goes on to observe that: ". . . the impact of directive leadership upon subordinates is

---

[79] Douglas McGregor, "Notes on Organization Theory," unpublished manuscript, Massachusetts Institute of Technology, 1958, cited by Warren G. Bennis, "Leadership Theory and Administrative Behavior," *Administrative Science Quarterly*, Vol. 4, No. 3 (December, 1959), p. 262.

[80] Gouldner, *op. cit.*

similar to that which the formal organization has on sub-ordinates. Pressure-oriented directive leadership 'compounds the felony . . . ,' reinforces and perpetuates the damage created by the organization's structure." [81]

*It is this extreme form of leadership behavior and its consequent effects on the entire social system that characterized the plant studied here in its early period. In the middle stood the manager who had lost what Gouldner calls the "social connective tissue" with both subordinates and superiors; the new manager established a sustained acceptable relationship with both.*

If it can be assumed that, within limits, it is possible for a leader to perform two roles simultaneously—roles which are obviously quite different at times—then it is necessary, as the present study has tried to do, to find out more about the actions which trigger the process by which this accommodation is achieved.

What are the mechanisms by which the successful leader gets thing done? In a hierarchical organization those on top are in a position to receive more information and to issue more directives than those at lower levels. "The higher the rank the larger the number of persons that originate for the leader." [82]

There is a vast network of "accounting procedures" available to the leader. The man on top is in a position to know the *results* of performance, but a multilevel structure is not necessarily well suited to insuring a constant and reliable flow of information from below. The manager's first obligation is to carry out the company's mandate to produce; directives and procedures circumscribe what he can or cannot do. Since he is in a power position he can use actions sanctioned from above to punish deviant behavior; subordinates know this. There is a tendency, as Blau, Gouldner, Selznick, and Merton point out, for the head of the organization to rely on disciplinary powers. When he does so the organization becomes rigid with respect to upward communications. "Extreme rigidity in

---

[81] Argyris, *op. cit.*, p. 130.
[82] Homans, *op. cit.*, p. 141.

hierarchical organizations reveals that they are usually associated with fear of superiors." [83]

If a change is to be made, then the leader in his own actions must somehow institute mechanisms, other than those available to him in the formal organization, for finding out about and acting intelligently in response to matters which are important to those at lower levels. Industrial practitioners use such mechanisms every day, but we know almost nothing as to how they are instituted and maintained over time. It is hoped that the study of Plant Y has identified some of these mechanisms.

---

[83] Blau, *op. cit.*, p. 90.

# Bibliography

This bibliography includes references used in this study and a selected group of readings appropriate to the study of leadership, organization, and change.

ADAMS, RICHARD N., AND PREISS, JACK J. (eds.). *Human Organization Research*. Homewood, Ill.: Published for the Society for Applied Anthropology by The Dorsey Press, 1960.

ARENSBERG, CONRAD M. "Behavior and Organization: Industrial Studies," *Social Psychology at the Crossroads* (eds. JOHN H. ROHRER AND MUZAFER SHERIF). New York: Harper & Bros., 1951.

———, AND McGREGOR, DOUGLAS. "Determination of Morale in an Industrial Company," *Applied Anthropology*, Vol. 1, No. 2 (January–March, 1942), pp. 12–34.

———. "Industry and Community," *American Journal of Sociology*, Vol. 27, No. 4 (July, 1942).

———, AND CHAPPLE, ELIOT D. *Measuring Human Relations*. (Genetic Psychology Monographs, Vol. 22, No. 1.) Provincetown, Mass.: The Journal Press, 1940.

———, AND TOOTELL, GEOFFREY. "Plant Sociology: Real Dimensions and New Problems," *Common Frontiers of the Social Sciences* (ed. Mirra Komarovsky). Glencoe, Ill.: Free Press, 1957.

———, AND HORSFALL, A. B. "Teamwork and Productivity in a Shoe Factory, *Human Organization*, Vol. 8, No. 1 (Winter, 1949), pp. 13–25.

ARGYRIS, CHRIS. *Executive Leadership*. New York: Harper & Bros., 1952.

———. "The Individual and Organization: Some Problems of Mutual Adjustment," *Administrative Science Quarterly*, Vol. 2, No. 1 (June, 1957), pp. 1–24.

———. "Organizational Leadership and Participative Management," *Journal of Business of the University of Chicago*, Vol. 28, No. 1 (January, 1955), pp. 1–7.

———. *Personality and Organization*. New York: Harper & Bros., 1957.

161

————. *The Present State of Human Relations Research*. New Haven: Labor and Management Center, Yale University, 1954.

————. *Understanding Organizational Behavior*. Homewood, Ill.: The Dorsey Press, 1960.

BAKKE, E. WIGHT. *Adaptive Human Behavior*. New Haven: Labor and Management Center, Yale University, 1947.

————. *Bonds of Organization*. New York: Harper & Bros., 1950.

————. *The Fusion Process*. New Haven: Labor and Management Center, Yale University, 1955.

————. *Organization and the Individual*. New Haven: Labor and Management Center, Yale University, 1952.

————, AND ARGYRIS, CHRIS. *Organizational Structure and Dynamics*. New Haven: Labor and Management Center, Yale University, 1955.

BARBER, BERNARD. "Structural-Functional Analysis: Some Problems and Misunderstandings," *American Sociological Review*, Vol. 21, No. 2 (April, 1956), pp. 129–35.

BARNARD, CHESTER I. *The Functions of the Executive*. Cambridge, Mass.: Harvard University Press, 1938.

————. *Organization and Management*. Cambridge, Mass.: Harvard University Press, 1948.

BARNES, LOUIS B. *Organizational Systems and Engineering Groups*. Boston, Mass.: Harvard University, Graduate School of Business Administration, Division of Research, 1960.

BARTON, A. AND LAZARSFELD, PAUL. "The Role of Qualitative Analysis in Social Research," *Frankfurter Beitraege zur Soziologie*. Frankfurt: Europaeische Verlagsanstalt, 1955.

BASS, BERNARD M. *Leadership, Psychology, and Organizational Behavior*. New York: Harper & Bros., 1960.

BENDIX, REINHARD. "Bureaucracy: The Problem and Its Setting," *American Sociological Review*, Vol. 12, No. 4 (August, 1947), pp. 493–507.

————. *Work and Authority in Industry*. New York: John Wiley & Sons, Inc., 1956.

BENNIS, WARREN G. "Leadership Theory and Administrative Behavior," *Administrative Science Quarterly*, Vol. 4, No. 3 (December, 1959), pp. 259–301.

BLAU, PETER M. *Bureaucracy in Modern Society*. New York: Random House, 1956.

————. "Formal Organization: Dimensions of Analysis," *American Journal of Sociology*, Vol. 63, No. 1 (July, 1957), pp. 58–69.

BROWN, ALVIN. *Organization of Industry*. Englewood Cliffs, N. J.: Prentice-Hall, Inc., 1947.

Brown, J. A. C. *The Social Psychology of Industry*. Harmondsworth, Middlesex, England: Penguin Books, Ltd., 1954.

Burlingame, Roger. *Backgrounds of Power*. New York: Charles Scribner's Sons, 1949.

Chapple, Eliot D., and Coon, Carleton. *Principles of Anthropology*. New York: Henry Holt & Co., Inc., 1942.

——, and Sayles, Leonard R. *The Measure of Management*. New York: Macmillan Co., 1961.

Chinoy, Ely. *Automobile Workers and the American Dream*. Garden City, New York: Doubleday & Co., Inc., 1955.

Chowdhry, Kamla, and Newcomb, Theodore M. "The Relative Abilities of Leaders and Non-Leaders to Estimate Opinions of Their Own Groups," *Journal of Abnormal and Social Psychology*, Vol. 47, No. 1 (January, 1952), pp. 51–57.

Coch, Lester, and French, John R. P., Jr., "Overcoming Resistance to Change," *Human Relations*, Vol. 1, No. 4 (1948), pp. 512–32.

Copeland, Melvin T. *The Executive at Work*. Cambridge, Mass.: Harvard University Press, 1952.

Dale, Ernest, and Urwick, Lyndall F. *Staff in Organization*. New York: McGraw-Hill Book Co., 1960.

Dalton, Melville. "Conflicts between Staff and Line Managerial Officers," *American Sociological Review*, Vol. 15, No. 3 (June, 1950), pp. 342–56.

——. *Men Who Manage*. New York: John Wiley & Sons, Inc., 1959.

——, Collins, O., and Roy, D. "Restrictions of Output and Social Cleavage in Industry," *Applied Anthropology*, Vol. 5, No. 3 (Summer, 1946).

Dennison, Henry S. *Organization Engineering*. New York: McGraw-Hill Book Co., 1931.

Eisenstadt, S. N. "Bureaucracy, Bureaucratization, and Debureaucratization," *Administrative Science Quarterly*, Vol. 4, No. 3 (December, 1959), pp. 302–20.

Ellsworth, John S. *Factory Folkways*. New Haven: Yale University Press, 1952.

Etzioni, Amatai (ed.). *Complex Organizations: A Sociological Reader*. New York: Holt, Rhinehart, & Winston, Inc., 1961.

Fayol, Henri. *General and Industrial Management*. New York: Pitman Publishing Corp., 1949.

Fleishman, Edwin A. "Leadership Climate, Human Relations Training and Supervisory Behavior," *Personnel Psychology*, Vol. 6, No. 1 (Summer, 1953), pp. 205–22.

FLEISHMAN, E. A., BURTT, W. E., and HARRIS, E. F. *Leadership and Supervision in Industry: An Evaluation of a Supervisory Training Program.* (Monograph No. 33.) Columbus, Ohio: Bureau of Educational Research, 1955.

FRIEDMANN, GEORGES. *Problemes Humaines du Machinisme Industrial.* Paris: Gallimard, 1946.

GIBB, CECIL A. "Leadership," *Handbook of Social Psychology* (ed. GARDNER LINDZEY), pp. 877–920. Cambridge, Mass.: Addison-Wesley Publishing Co., Inc., 1954.

GINSBERG, ELI, AND REILLY, EWING W. *Effecting Change in Large Organizations.* New York: Columbia University Press, 1957.

———. *What Makes an Executive.* New York: Columbia University Press, 1955.

GOLDEN, CLINTON S., AND RUTTENBERG, HAROLD J. *The Dynamics of an Industrial Democracy.* New York: Harper & Bros., 1942.

GORDON, ROBERT A. *Business Leadership in the Large Corporation.* Washington, D.C.: Brookings Institution, 1945.

GOULDNER, ALVIN W. "Organizational Analysis," *Sociology Today— Problems and Prospects* (eds. ROBERT K. MERTON, LEONARD BROOM, AND LEONARD S. COTTRELL, JR.), pp. 400–428. New York: Basic Books, Inc., 1959.

———. *Patterns of Industrial Bureaucracy.* Glencoe, Ill.: Free Press, 1954.

———. *Studies in Leadership.* New York: Harper & Bros., 1950.

———. *Wildcat Strike.* Yellow Springs, Ohio: Antioch Press, 1954.

* GUEST, ROBERT H. "Categories of Events in Field Observations," *Human Organization Research* (ed. R. N. ADAMS AND J. J. PREISS). Homewood, Ill.: Dorsey Press, 1960.

———. "Foremen at Work—An Interim Report on Method," *Human Organization,* Vol. 14, No. 2 (Summer, 1955), pp. 21–25.

———. "Job Enlargement—A Revolution in Job Design," *Personnel Administration,* Vol. 20, No. 2 (March-April, 1957), pp. 9–16.

———. "Men and Machines," *Personnel,* Vol. 31, No. 6 (May, 1955), pp. 496–503.

———. "A Neglected Factor in Labour Turnover," *Occupational Psychology,* Vol. 29, No. 4 (October, 1955), pp. 217–31.

———. "Of Time and the Foreman," *Personnel,* Vol. 32, No. 6 (May, 1956), pp. 478–96.

———. "Work Careers and Aspirations of Automobile Workers," *American Sociological Review,* Vol. 19, No. 2 (April, 1954), pp. 155–63.

GULICK, LUTHER, AND URWICK, LYNDALL F. *Papers on the Science of*

*Administration.* New York: Institute of Public Administration, 1937.

HAIRE, MASON (ed). *Modern Organization Theory.* New York: John Wiley & Sons, Inc., 1959.

HALPIN, A. W., AND WINER, B. J. *The Leadership Behavior of the Airplane Commander.* Columbus, Ohio: The Ohio State University Research Foundation, 1952.

HAYTHORN, WILLIAM, COUCH, A. S., et al. "The Behavior of Authoritarian and Egalitarian Personalities in Groups," *Human Relations,* Vol. 9, No. 1 (February, 1956), pp. 57–74.

HOMANS, GEORGE C. *The Human Group.* New York: Harcourt, Brace & Co., 1950.

————. *Social Behavior: Its Elementary Forms.* New York: Harcourt, Brace & World, 1961.

HUGHES, EVERETT C. *Men and Their Work.* Glencoe, Ill.: Free Press, 1958.

JACOBSON, EUGENE, CHARTERS, JR., W. W., AND LIEBERMAN, SEYMOUR. "The Use of the Role Concept in the Study of Complex Organization," *Journal of Social Issues,* Vol. 7, No. 3 (1951), pp. 18–27.

JACQUES, ELIOT. *The Changing Culture of a Factory.* New York: Dryden Press, 1952.

* JASINSKI, FRANK J. "Adapting Organization to New Technology," *Harvard Business Review,* Vol. 37, No. 1 (January–February, 1959), pp. 79–86.

————. "The Dynamics of Organizational Behavior," *Personnel,* Vol. 36, No. 3 (March–April, 1959), pp. 32–40.

————. "Status and Role of Assembly Line Foremen." Unpublished Ph.D. dissertation, Department of Anthropology, Yale University, 1955.

————, AND GUEST, ROBERT H., "Redesigning the Supervisor's Job," *Factory Management and Maintenance,* Vol. 115, No. 12 (December, 1957).

KAHN, ROBERT L., AND KATZ, DANIEL. "Leadership Practices in Relation to Productivity and Morale," *Group Dynamics: Research and Theory* (eds. D. CARTWRIGHT AND A. ZANDER). Evanston, Ill.: Row, Peterson, & Co., 1953.

————, AND MORSE, NANCY C. "The Relationship of Productivity to Morale," *Journal of Social Issues,* Vol. 7, No. 3 (1951), pp. 8–17.

KALLEJIAN, VERNE J., WESCHLER, IRVING R., AND TANNENBAUM, ROBERT. "Managers in Transition," *Harvard Business Review,* Vol. 33, No. 4 (July–August, 1955), pp. 55–64.

KATZ, DANIEL. Introduction to "Human Relations Research in Large Organizations," *Journal of Social Issues,* Vol. 7, No. 3 (1951), pp. 4–7.

KATZ, ELIHU, AND LAZARSFELD, PAUL F. *Personal Influence: The Part*

*Played by People in the Flow of Mass Communication.* Glencoe, Ill.: Free Press, 1955.

KINGSLEY, J. DONALD. *Representative Bureaucracy.* Yellow Springs, Ohio: Antioch Press, 1944.

KROEBER, A. L. "Critical Summary and Commentary," *Method and Perspective in Anthropology* (ed. ROBERT F. SPENCER). Minneapolis, Minn.: University of Minnesota Press, 1954.

LAWRENCE, PAUL R. *The Changing of Organizational Behavior Patterns: A Case Study of Decentralization.* Boston, Mass.: Harvard University, Graduate School of Business Administration, Division of Research, 1958.

LAZARSFELD, PAUL, AND THIELENS, JR., W. *The Academic Mind.* Glencoe, Ill.: Free Press, 1958.

————, AND ROSENBERG, N. (eds.). *The Language of Social Research.* Glencoe, Ill.: Free Press, 1955.

————. "Problems in Methodology," *Sociology Today—Problems and Prospects* (eds. ROBERT K. MERTON, LEONARD BROOM, AND LEONARD S. COTTRELL, JR.). New York: Basic Books, Inc., 1959.

————. "Reflections on Business," *American Journal of Sociology,* Vol. 65, No. 1 (July, 1959), pp. 1–31.

LEAVITT, HAROLD J. "Small Groups in Large Organizations," *Journal of Business of the University of Chicago,* Vol. 28, No. 1 (January, 1955), pp. 8–17.

LEIGHTON, ALEXANDER H. *Human Relations in a Changing World.* New York: E. P. Dutton & Co., Inc., 1949.

LEMKE, BERNHARD C., AND EDWARDS, JAMES D. (eds.). *Administrative Control and Executive Action.* Columbus, Ohio: C. E. Merrill Books, 1961.

LEWIN, K. "Group Decision and Social Change," *Readings in Social Psychology* (eds. E. E. MACCOBY, E. L. HARTLEY, AND T. M. NEWCOMB). New York: Henry Holt & Co., Inc., 1958.

LIKERT, R. "Developing Patterns in Management," *General Management Series No. 78.* New York: American Management Association, 1955.

LIPPITT, RONALD, WATSON, JEANNE, AND WESLEY, BRUCE. *The Dynamics of Planned Change.* New York: Harcourt, Brace & Co., 1958.

————, AND WHITE, R. K. "The Social Climate of Children's Groups," *Child Behavior and Development* (eds. R. G. BARKER, J. S. KOUNIN, AND H. F. WHYTE), pp. 485–508. New York: McGraw-Hill Book Co., 1943.

LYND, ROBERT S., AND LYND, HELEN M. *Middletown in Transition.* New York: Harcourt, Brace & Co., 1939.

MCGREGOR, DOUGLAS. "Conditions of Effective Leadership in the Industrial Organization," *Journal of Consulting Psychology*, Vol. 8, No. 2 (March–April, 1944), pp. 55–63.

————. *The Human Side of Enterprise*. New York: McGraw-Hill Book Co., 1960.

————. "Notes on Organization Theory." Unpublished manuscript, Massachusetts Institute of Technology, 1958. Cited by Warren G. Bennis, "Leadership Theory and Administrative Behavior," *Administrative Science Quarterly*, Vol. 4, No. 3 (December, 1959), pp. 259–301.

MAIN, T. AND NYSANDER, M. "Some Observations on Training-Groups." Unpublished manuscript, Bethel, Maine, 1951. Cited by W. G. Bennis, "Leadership Theory and Administrative Behavior," *Administrative Science Quarterly*, Vol. 4, No. 3 (December, 1959), pp. 259–301.

MALINOWSKI, BRONISLAW. *A Scientific Theory of Culture*. Chapel Hill, N. C.: University of North Carolina Press, 1944.

MANN, FLOYD C. "Changing Superior-Subordinate Relationships," *Journal of Social Issues*, Vol. 7, No. 3 (1951), pp. 56–63.

————. "Studying and Creating Change: A Means to Understanding Social Organization," *Research in Industrial Human Relations* (eds. C. M. ARENSBERG *et al.*). New York: Harper & Bros., 1957.

————, AND DENT, JAMES K. "The Supervisor: Member of Two Organizational Families," *Harvard Business Review*, Vol. 32, No. 6 (November–December, 1954), pp. 103–12.

————, AND NEFF, FRANKLIN W. *Managing Major Change in Organizations*. Ann Arbor, Mich.: Foundation for Research on Human Behavior, 1961.

MARCH, JAMES G., AND SIMON, H. A. (with the collaboration of HAROLD GUETZKOW). *Organizations*. New York: John Wiley & Sons, Inc., 1958.

MERTON, ROBERT K. "Bureaucratic Structure and Personality," *Social Forces*, Vol. 18, No. 4 (May, 1940), pp. 560–68.

————, AND LAZARSFELD, PAUL F. (eds.). *Continuities in Social Research: Studies in the Scope and Method of the American Soldier*. Glencoe, Ill.: Free Press, 1950.

————. *Social Theory and Social Structure* (rev. ed.). Glencoe, Ill.: Free Press, 1957.

MILLER, FRANK B. *Expanding the Scope of Case Study Research by Interaction Counting*. Ithaca, N. Y.: Cornell University (mimeographed), 1953.

————. "Situational Interactions—A Worthwhile Concept?" *Human Organization*, Vol. 17, No. 4 (Winter, 1958–1959), pp. 37–47.

MILLS, C. WRIGHT. *White Collar*. New York: Oxford University Press, 1953.

MOORE, WILBERT E. "Industrial Sociology: Status and Prospects," *American Sociological Review,* Vol. 13, No. 4 (August, 1948), pp. 382–91.

———. *Industrial Relations and the Social Order* (rev. ed.). New York: Macmillan Co., 1951.

MORENO, JACOB L. *Who Shall Survive?* (rev. ed.). Beacon, N. Y.: Beacon House, 1953.

MORSE, NANCY C., AND REIMER, EVERETT. "The Experimental Change of a Major Organizational Variable," *Journal of Abnormal and Social Psychology,* Vol. 52, No. 1 (January, 1956), pp. 120–29.

NEWCOMB, THEODORE M. "Social Psychological Theory: Integrating Individual and Social Approaches," *Social Psychology at the Crossroads* (eds. JOHN H. ROHRER AND MUZAFER SHERIF). New York: Harper & Bros., 1951.

PARSONS, TALCOTT. "Suggestions for a Sociological Theory of Organization," *Administrative Science Quarterly,* Vol. 1, No. 1 (June, 1956), pp. 63–85.

PELZ, DONALD C. "Leadership within a Hierarchical Organization," *Journal of Social Issues,* Vol. 7, No. 3 (1951), pp. 49–55.

RICE, A. K. "The Experimental Reorganization on Non-Automatic Weaving in an Indian Mill," *Human Relations,* Vol. 8, No. 3 (August, 1955), pp. 199–249.

* RICHARDSON, FREDERICK L. W., AND WALKER, CHARLES R. *Human Relations in an Expanding Company.* New Haven: Labor and Management Center, Yale University, 1948.

———. *Talk, Work, and Action.* (Monograph No. 3, 1961.) Published by The Society for Applied Anthropology, Cornell University, Ithaca, New York.

RIEKEN, HENRY W., AND HOMANS, GEORGE C. "Psychological Aspects of Social Structure," *Handbook of Social Psychology,* Vol. II (ed. GARDNER LINDZEY). Cambridge, Mass.: Addison-Wesley Publishing Co., Inc., 1954.

ROETHLISBERGER, FRITZ J. "The Foreman: Master and Victim of Double Talk," *Harvard Business Review,* Vol. 23, No. 3 (Spring, 1945), pp. 283–98.

———, AND DICKSON, WILLIAM. *Management and the Worker.* Cambridge, Mass.: Harvard University Press, 1939.

ROGERS, CARL. *Client-Centered Therapy.* Boston, Mass.: Houghton-Mifflin Co., 1951.

RONKEN, HARRIET O., AND LAWRENCE, PAUL R. *Administering Changes: A Case Study of Human Relations in a Factory.* Boston, Mass.: Harvard University, Graduate School of Business Administration, Division of Research, 1956.

RUBENSTEIN, ALBERT H., AND HABERSTROH, CHADWICK J. (eds.). *Some Theories of Organization*. Homewood, Ill.: Irwin–Dorsey Press, 1960.

SANFORD, FILLMORE H. "The Follower's Role in Leadership Phenomena," *Readings in Social Psychology* (eds. GUY E. SWANSON, THEODORE M. NEWCOMB, AND EUGENE L. HARTLEY). New York: Henry Holt & Co., Inc., 1952.

SARGENT, S. STANSFIELD. "Conceptions of Role and Ego in Contemporary Psychology," *Social Psychology at the Crossroads* (eds. JOHN H. ROHRER AND MUZAFER SHERIF). New York: Harper & Bros., 1951.

SAYLES, LEONARD R. *Behavior of Industrial Work Groups*. New York: John Wiley & Sons, Inc., 1958.

———. "A Case Study of Union Participation and Technological Change," *Human Organization*, Vol. 11, No. 1 (Spring, 1952), pp. 5–15.

———. "Human Relations and the Organization of Work," *Michigan Business Review*, Vol. 6 (1954), pp. 21–25.

———, AND STRAUSS, GEORGE. *The Local Union*. New York: Harper & Bros., 1953.

SELZNICK, PHILIP. "Foundations of the Theory of Organization," *American Sociological Review*, Vol. 8, No. 1 (February, 1948), pp. 25–35.

———. *TVA and the Grass Roots*. Berkeley and Los Angeles, Calif.: University of California, 1949.

SHERIF, MUZAFER. "Introduction," *Social Psychology at the Crossroads* (eds. JOHN M. ROHRER AND MUZAFER SHERIF). New York: Harper & Bros., 1951.

SIMON, HERBERT. *Administrative Behavior*. New York: Macmillan Co., 1948.

———. *The New Science of Management Decision*. New York: Harper & Bros., 1960.

STOGDILL, RALPH M. *Individual Behavior and Group Achievement*. New York: Oxford University Press, 1959.

———. "Personal Factors Associated with Leadership: A Survey of the Literature," *Journal of Psychology*, Vol. 25 (1948), pp. 35–71.

STRAUSS, GEORGE, AND SAYLES, LEONARD R. *Personnel: The Human Problems of Management*. Englewood Cliffs, N. J.: Prentice-Hall, Inc., 1960.

SUOJANEN, WAINO W. "Leadership, Authority and the Span of Control," *Advanced Management*, Vol. 22, No. 9 (September, 1957), pp. 17–22.

TANNENBAUM, ARNOLD S., AND KAHN, ROBERT L. *Organizational Control Structure*. Unpublished manuscript, University of Michigan Survey Research Center, November, 1955.

TANNENBAUM, ROBERT, WESCHLER, IRVING R., AND MASSARIK, FRED. *Leadership and Organization*. New York: McGraw-Hill Book Co., 1961.

TAYLOR, DONALD W., BERRY, PAUL, AND BLOCK, CLIFFORD H. "Group Participation, Brainstorming, and Creative Thinking, "*Administrative Science Quarterly*, Vol. 3, No. 1 (June, 1958), pp. 24–47.

TAYLOR, FREDERICK W. *Scientific Management.* New York: Harper & Bros., 1948.

* TURNER, ARTHUR N. "Impersonality and Group Membership—A Case Study of an Automobile Assembly Line." Unpublished Ph.D. Thesis, Cornell University, September, 1958.

———. "Management and the Assembly Line," *Harvard Business Review*, Vol. 33, No. 5 (September–October, 1955), pp. 40–48.

URWICK, LYNDALL F. *The Elements of Administration.* New York: Harper & Bros., 1944.

VITELES, M. S. *Motivation and Morale in Industry.* New York: W. W. Norton & Co., Inc., 1953.

* WALKER, CHARLES R., GUEST, ROBERT H., AND TURNER, ARTHUR N. *The Foreman on the Assembly Line.* Cambridge, Mass.: Harvard University Press, 1956.

———, AND GUEST, ROBERT H. *The Man on the Assembly Line.* Cambridge, Mass.: Harvard University Press, 1952.

———. *Modern Technology and Civilization.* New York: McGraw-Hill Book Co., 1962.

———. *Steeltown.* New York: Harper & Bros., 1950.

———. *Toward the Automatic Factory.* New Haven: Yale University Press, 1957.

WARNER, W. LLOYD, et al. *The Social System of the Modern Factory.* New Haven: Yale University Press, 1947.

WEBER, MAX. *Essays in Sociology* (eds. and trans. H. H. GERTH AND C. WRIGHT MILLS), New York: Oxford University Press, 1946.

———. *The Theory of Social and Economic Organization* (trans. A. H. HENDERSON, and ed. TALCOTT PARSONS). New York: Oxford University Press, 1947.

WEISS, ROBERT S. *Processes of Organization.* (Survey Research Series, Publication no. 17.) Ann Arbor, Mich.: University of Michigan, Institute for Social Research, Survey Research Center, 1956.

WHYTE, WILLIAM F. "Framework for the Analysis of Industrial Relations," *Industrial and Labor Relations Review:* Vol. 3, No. 3 (April, 1950), pp. 393–401.

———. *Human Relations in the Restaurant Industry.* New York: McGraw-Hill Book Co., 1948.

———. *Leadership and Group Participation.* Bulletin No. 24, Ithaca,

N. Y.: New York State School of Industrial and Labor Relations, Cornell University, May, 1953.

―――. *Man and Organization: Three Problems in Human Relations in Industry.* Homewood, Ill.: Richard D. Irwin, Inc., 1959.

―――. *Pattern for Industrial Peace.* New York: Harper & Bros., 1951.

WHYTE, JR., WILLIAM H. *The Organization Man.* New York: Simon and Schuster, Inc., 1956.

YOUMANN, E. GRANT. "The Administrative Mind," *Public Personnel Review,* Vol. 15, No. 2 (April, 1954), pp. 62–76.

ZALEZNIK, A. *Foreman Training in a Growing Enterprise.* Boston, Mass.: Harvard University, Graduate School of Business Administration, Division of Research, 1951.

―――, CHRISTENSEN, C. R. AND ROETHLISBERGER, F. J. *The Motivation, Productivity, and Satisfaction of Workers: A Prediction Study.* With the Assistance and Collaboration of George C. Homans. Boston, Mass.: Harvard University, Graduate School of Business Administration, Division of Research, 1958.

ZNANIECKI, FLORIAN. *The Social Role of the Man of Knowledge.* New York: Columbia University Press, 1940.

---

* Authors marked with an asterisk (*) were members of the Yale Technology Project; Charles R. Walker, Director, and Robert H. Guest, Associate Director.

# Author Index

## A

Arensberg, C. M., 2, 3, 83, 148, 151–53, 156
Argyris, C., 3, 141, 143–45, 149, 159

## B

Bakke, E. W., 2, 144, 150
Bamforth, K. W., 136
Barber, B., 153
Barnard, C. I., 131, 157
Bennis, W. G., 118, 120–21
Blau, P. M., 3, 147, 159
Brown, A., 141
Brown, J. A. C., 154
Burlingame, R., 140
Burtt, W. E., 96

## C

Chapple, E. D., 83, 131
Charters, W. W., Jr., 143
Coch, L., 104, 152
Coon, C., 83
Couch, A. S., 156

## D

Dalton, M., 150
Dennison, H. S., 141
Dickson, W., 148

## E

Ellsworth, J. S., 143–44, 150

## F

Fayol, H., 141
Fleishman, E. A., 96, 156
French, J. R. P., Jr., 104, 152

## G

Gibb, C. A., 157
Ginsberg, E., 150
Gouldner, A. W., 3, 120–21, 124–25, 147–48, 150, 158–59
Guest, R. H., 13, 84, 119, 129
Gulick, L., 141

## H

Haire, M., 1, 7, 107
Halpin, A. W., 155
Harris, E. F., 96
Haythorn, W., 156
Homans, G. C., 3, 82–83, 92, 151, 156, 159

## J

Jacobson, E., 143
Jacques, E., 149–50
Jasinski, F. J., 129

## K

Kahn, R. L., 144
Katz, D., 145
Kroeber, A. L., 149

## L

Lazarsfeld, P. F., 153
Leavitt, H., 152
Leighton, A. H., 151
Lieberman, S., 143
Likert, R., 119
Lippitt, R., 150, 156

## M

Main, T., 121
Malinowski, B., 143
Mann, F. C., 150
March, J. G., 2
McGregor, D., 122–24, 127, 158
Merton, R. K., 107, 121, 140–42, 146, 151, 156–57, 159
Moreno, J. L., 121
Morse, N. C., 144

## N

Newcomb, T. M., 152
Nysander, W., 121

## P

Parsons, T., 2
Pelz, D. C., 157

**R**

Reilly, E. W., 150
Rice, A. K., 150
Richardson, F. L. W., 83
Rieken, H. W., 151
Roethlisberger, F., 148
Rogers, C., 121

**S**

Sanford, F. H., 155
Sargent, S. S., 144
Selznick, P., 159
Sherif, M., 151
Simon, H., 2
Stodgill, R. M., 155
Suojanen, W. W., 121, 145, 157

**T**

Taylor, F. W., 120, 140

**Tootell**, G., 3, 151, 153, 156
Trist, E. L., 136
Turner, A. N., 13, 119

**U**

Urwick, L. F., 141

**W**

Walker, C. R., 13, 83, 119, 150
Watson, J., 150
Weber, M., 122, 126, 141, 150
Wesley, B., 150
White, R. K., 156
Whyte, W. F., 83, 150
Winer, B. J., 155

**Z**

Znaniecki, F., 148

# Subject Index

## A

Absenteeism
  compared in two time periods, 103
  enforcement of rules of, 27–28
Activities, results of, measured by performance, 97
Assembly plants, 10
Attitudes
  favorable expression of, in Period II, 57–59
  slow change of, 58
Authority
  "classical" definition of, 120
  conditions of, 128–33
  criterion used to measure, 119
  definition of, 118–19, 156–57
  "human relations" definition of, 121
  nature of, 118–33 *passim*
  "revisionist" definition of, 121–23
  summary observations about Plant Y, 126–27
Automobile industry, conditions in 1953, 17
Automobiles
  number produced at Plant Y, 13
  variety of specifications, 14–15

## B

Bureaucracy, defined by Weber and Merton, 141–42
Bureaucratic functions, and leadership, 3

## C

Capital investment, and "payoff" proof, 50
Car conditioning department, 14
Chain of command, principle of, 141
Change agent, role of, 118
Change process, dependency on external conditions, 114–15
Chassis department, 14
"Chewing out," effects of, 23
Communications
  through chain of command, 24
  on formal organization chart, 33
  pattern in Period I, 19

Competition, 18
  interplant, 19
Comprehensive framework, need for, in organization theory, 2
Comptroller
  functions of, 10–11
  quote from, 78–81
  relation to, in Period II, 77–81
Conflict, reduction linked to improved operations, 124
Controls
  effects of accounting, 78–79
  effects compared in two time periods, 72
  and work standards, 75
Conveyor, description of, 13–14
Cooley, Matthew, succession of, 41
Cooperation
  "centrally controlled," 24
  between departments increased, 65
Coordination, in assembly operations, 31
Corporate policies, restrictions of, 12
Corporation size, 9
Culture, an influence on in-plant behavior, 148–49

## D

Decentralization, corporate policy of, 12
Decision making
  comptroller's role in, 81
  function of staff in, 45
  and interaction patterns, 88
  involvement of subordinates in, 131
  at lower levels, 62–63 *passim*, 77, 112–13
  process of in Period I, 32
  process of in Period II, 69
  on technical changes, 52
Deductive approach, 7
Development, continuous adjustive, 3
Directives
  carrying out, 18
  ignored in Period I, 21
  issued by superiors, 32

Discharge, not used as disciplinary weapon, 47–48
Discipline
concept of, 142
effects of, 159–60
Disintegration
at Plant Y, 17–39
spiral effect of, 134–35
Division manager, responsibilities of, 10
Dual role
concept of, 124, 158
exercised by new manager, 125
political function of, 128
Dysfunction
Plant Y example of, 107
source of, 146

**E**

Efficiency
loss and recovery during schedule change, 98
in periods of model change, 100–101
of Plant Y in Period II, 98–99
Efficiency reports
calculation of, 79
misunderstood, 78
Emergencies
effects of, 21, 29, 43
effects of new material controls in reducing, 68
elimination of, 113
reduction of, with new technical changes, 54
Executive vice-president, quote from, 40–41
Expertise, defined by Gouldner, 124

**F**

Fear
of efficiency figures, 78
elimination of, 58
as primary motivation, 22, 25
Foremen
"in the middle," 26–27
invitation of manager to, 42
quotes from, 24, 26, 29–30, 35–37, 49, 55, 61–65, 68, 70, 72–74
relation to hourly workers in Period I, 30
relation to manager in Period I, 23–24
relation to manager in Period II, 59–60
relation to superiors in Period I, 25–30 *passim*
relation to superiors in Period II, 61–63

Formal organization
and conflict with needs of subordinates, 143–49 *passim*
definition of, 138
rational principles applied to, 140–41
Formal organization effectiveness, criterion of, 144
Formal structure, not primary change factor, 116–17
Friction, sources of, 26
Fusion process, 150

**G**

General foremen
quotes from, 22–23, 25–26, 29, 33, 41–42, 46, 52, 54, 59, 64
relation to manager in Period I, 22–23
relation to manager in Period II, 59–60
Goal attainment, collaborative process of, 122
Goals, convergence of, 2
Grievances, record in two time periods, 102
Group interaction, as condition of authority, 131–33
Group meetings
effects on interpersonal relations, 47
effects on sentiments, 95
and elimination of inspection problems, 70
for improving physical plant, 50
informally established at lower levels, 46–47
of manager in Period I, 20–21
of manager in Period II, 44–46
and new role of plant engineering, 76
stabilizing effect of, 86–87
as vehicle of authority, 132–33
Group norms, and leadership, 157
Group reinforcement, tension and stress modified by, 151–52

**H**

Human relations
"just talk," 23
question of training in, 96

**I**

Impersonality
in a bureaucracy, 145
concept of, 142
Individual, worth of, stressed by new manager, 60
Inductive approach, 7

Informal organization, neglected in bureaucracy, 145
Inspection
    conflicts within, 36
    functions of, 11
    relation to, in Period I, 34–37
    relation to, in Period II, 69–71
Integration, of perceptions in target setting, 123
Interaction
    with comptroller, 91
    crisis effects of, 87
    definition of, 83
    direction of, 84
    frequency of, 84–85
    with inspection, 90
    institutionalizing, as phase of change, 110
    patterns of, 82–92 passim
    among peers, 88–89
    production to nonproduction, 89–91
    in "set events," 86
    summary of, 91
    vertical, 85–89
    with work standards, 90
Interdependence, and effective authority, 123

J

Job assignments, shifts in, 47–49
Job security, as critical need for supervisors, 28

K

Korean War, effects on automobile production, 17

L

Labor costs
    comparison of indirect, 101
    reduction of, 98
Leader, role in change process, 154–60 passim
Leadership
    behavior characteristics of, 155-56
    effects of directive, 158
    a patterned social relationship, 156
    punishment-centered, 158
"Leeway to act," as condition of authority, 128
Level skipping, harmful effects of, 27
Line balance, effects of poor, 25
Line management, titles of, 9
Loyalty, conflict of, 30

M

Mass production
    definition of, 139
    principles of, 15
Material control
    changes in, 53
    elimination of shortages in, 66
    functions of, 11
    relation to, in Period I, 31–33
    relation to, in Period II, 66–69
Material flow, stoppage in, 21
Material shortages, effects of, 33
Mechanical breakdowns, effects of, on interpersonal relations, 15–16
Metal department, 14
    changes in, 52
Model building, 2
Moving equilibrium, 3

N

Needs, related to change phases, 109–10
Nonproduction departments
    relation to production in Period I, 31–37
    relation to production in Period II, 65–81
Norms, congruence of, among superiors and subordinates, 97

O

Orders
    confusion of, in inspection, 69
    effects of issuing, 30, 56
    legitimacy, questioned in Period I, 26, 35
Organization, principles of, summarized, 142
Organization research, problems of, 3–4
Organization theory, need for time dimension in, 2–3
Organizational change
    aftermath phase at Plant Y, 114
    being informed about needs as phase of, 109–10
    critical conditions leading to, 106–7
    cultural norms as condition of, 117
    enlarging span of cognition as phase in, 111–12
    and formal structure, 116–17
    institutionalizing interactions as phase of, 110
    internal inability to generate, 107
    length of time to effect, 115–16
    new field of enquiry, 1–2
    phases in process of, 107–14
    planning as phase of, 112–13
    process of, 106–17 passim

Organizational change—*Cont.*
  reduction of pressure as phase in, 108
  rejection of "factor" approach in, 150–51
  success reinforcement as phase in, 113–14
  technical change as phase of, 110–11
Organizational functions
  effects of separating, 131
  separation of, accented in Period I, 35–36
  separation of, minimized in Period II,
    70–71, 74, 76–77, 111
Organizational requirements, and needs of
  subordinates, 143–45
Organizational structure, at Plant Y, 9–13

**P**

Paint department, 14
  changes in, 51
Participation
  as change mechanism, 110
  tension and stress reduced through, 152
Peer relations, at foreman level in Period II,
  64
Perception
  conflicts in, 25–26
  of corporate decisions, 108
  of foremen to inspectors, 71
  of new manager's role by subordinates,
    57–60
  of nonproduction role change, 95–96
  of personality traits in two time periods,
    96
  as related to technical conditions, 135
  of subordinates' needs, 123
  of union toward new manager, 43
Performance
  as criterion of effective authority, 122
  low record in Period I, 37–39
  related to interaction-sentiment pattern,
    104
  slow improvement of, 109
  summary of, 103
  superior record in Period II, 97–103
Personality development, and organization
  requirements, 149
Personality traits
  constancy of, 96
  of new manager, 125–26
  rejected as useful change concept, 154
Personnel
  ratio of production to nonproduction, 15
  shifts in, 47–49
Personnel director, functions of, 11

Planning
  effects of technical changes on, 54
  lack of, in Period I, 20–21, 37
  in material control activities, 68
  as phase of change, 112–13
  positive sentiments about, 94
  as primary requirement at Plant Y, 43–44
Plant engineer
  functions of, 11
  quotes from, 53, 76
Plant engineering, relation to, in Period II,
  75–77
Plant formal organization, no changes in,
  under both managers, 13
Plant manager
  contacts in Period I, 20
  decision to replace, 40–42
  and division relationships in Period I, 17–
    20, 106
  introduction of new, 41–42
  limits on authority of, 12
  quotes from, 18–19, 43–44, 49, 67
  subordinates' relation to, in Period I, 20–
    24, 59
  subordinates' relation to, in Period II, 59–
    60
  succession of, 40–44, 107–8
  supported by corporation, 42
Plant operations
  changes introduced to improve, 51–55
  described, 13–16
  sensitivity to change in, 15–16
Plant Y, organization of, 10
Power, as distinguished from authority, 118
Powers, separation of, 35–36
Pressure
  from corporation in Period I, 18–20
  from division, 56
  internal versus external, 65
  as limiting authority, 126
  from manager to subordinates in Period I,
    22–23
  reduction of, as phase in change, 108
Primary groups, not in formal structure, 132
Process
  of change, 2, 106–17
  definition of, 139
Product, variety of, 14–15
Production, rate of, 13
Production schedules, effects of, 19
Profit, common goal of, 20
Promotions, encouragement of, by new manager, 48

## Q

Quality, versus quantity, 34
Quality performance, two time periods compared in, 101
Quality reports
negative effects of, 25–26
routing of, 34
Quantification, relationship patterns subject to, 105

## R

Rational structure, definition of, 138
Rationality, and predictability as basis of authority, 120
Regulations, effects of conformity to, 146–47
Representative leadership, of new manager, 125
Research procedures
controlling "constants" in, 5–6, 13
at Plant Y, 4–5
Roles, hierarchical, 144
Rule enforcement
effects of, 23
resented in Period I, 27–28
unanticipated consequences of, 147

## S

Safety performance, two time periods compared in, 101
Schedule changes, recovery from, 99
Scheduling, complex, in assembly operations, 15
Scientific management, and organization, 140
Sentiments
definition of, 92
discussion of, 92-97 passim
hostile expression of, in Period I, 93
toward nonproduction groups, 95
shift in, under new manager, 94–95, 108
Social change, origins of, 151–52
Socio-technical systems
origin of term, 135–36
and production organizations, 134–37
Span of cognition
as condition of authority, 130–31
enlargement of, as phase of change, 111–12
Span of control, principle of, 141
Specialization, principle of, 141
Spiral effect
of socio-technical problems, 135

Spiral effect—*Cont.*
of success, 113–14
of technical improvements, 54
Standardization, 15
Stewart, George, resignation of, 41
Subassembly operations, 14
Subordinates
fear of superiors by, in Period I, 107
viewed by superiors in Period II, 63–64
Success, and effect on change process, 113–14
Superintendents
quotes from, 20–22, 27–28, 33, 36, 46, 53, 58, 63, 68, 76
relation to manager in Period I, 21–22
Supervisory staff, 10
Suspicion, elimination of, 64, 76
Synchronized operations, 13

## T

Target setting, by leader, 123
Technical changes
introduced by new manager, 50–55
as phase of total change, 110–11
and sentiments, 94
Technical information, not exchanged in Period I, 36–37
Technology Project, previous research of, 4
Tension and stress
definition of, 139
general hypothesis, 153–54
in organization, 139–49 *passim*
Time
as crucial dimension of change, 153
patterns of change in, 3
Time dimension, in studies of change, 150
Time perspective, as condition of authority, 128–29
Trim department, 14
changes in, 53
Turnover, compared in two time periods, 103

## U

Understudies, need to develop, 48
Union committeeman
changes in work standards viewed by, 73
quotes from, 44, 51
Union officers, reaction to new manager, 43
Union president, quote from, 43
Unity of direction, principle of, 141

## V

Vertical relations
in Period I, 17–30
in Period II, 56–64

Vertical structure, and work flow interaction, 129–30

**W**

Walkout, and decision to remove manager, 40

Work assignments, determined by foremen, 72–73

Work flow
and effects on human relations, 52, 55
problems and effects of, 31

Work flow interaction, as condition of authority, 129–30

Work loads, determination of, by foremen, 74

Work standards
functions of, 11, 71–72
and policy of "keeping the clocks out," 73–74
relation to, in Period II, 71–75

Working conditions, first changes by new manager in, 50–51

*This book has been set on Intertype in 12 and 11 point Garamond, leaded 1 point. Chapter numbers are in 14 point and chapter titles in 24 point No. 315 Deepdene. The size of the type page is 25 by 42 picas.*